Presented To:

_____

From:

_____

Date:

_____

FREEDOM FIGHTER

FREEDOM FIGHTER

One Man's Fight for One
Free World

Majed El Shafie

DESTINY IMAGE® PUBLISHERS, INC.
P.O. Box 310, Shippensburg, PA 17257-0310
"Promoting Inspired Lives."

This book and all other Destiny Image, Revival Press, Mercy-Place, Fresh Bread, Destiny Image Fiction, and Treasure House books are available at Christian bookstores and distributors worldwide.

For a U.S. bookstore nearest you, call 1-800-722-6774.
For more information on foreign distributors, call 717-532-3040.
Reach us on the Internet: www.destinyimage.com.

ISBN 13 TP: 978-0-7684-0313-8
ISBN 13 Ebook: 978-0-7684-8773-2

For Worldwide Distribution, Printed in the U.S.A.
1 2 3 4 5 6 7 8 / 16 15 14 13 12

DEDICATION

To my mother, Samira, and my best friend, Tamir. You may have departed our world, but you will never leave my heart…

ACKNOWLEDGMENTS

I would like to thank my Lord and Savior for being there for me—always; every victim we have helped—each and every one of you has added something priceless to our lives and you remind us every day of why we put our lives on the line; Chris Atkins—thank you for your courage and support; Roberta and Grant Kurian—you are like family to me; Chantal Desloges—thank you for standing by the refugees; Mario Silva; Hon. Jason Kenney—you are a true champion for human rights; Sharon Harel—you stood beside me in the darkest time of my life; Li Xun (Falun Dafa Association of Canada); Barbara Crook (Palestinian Media Watch); Sid Roth; Lonnie Lane; Tim King; Anna-Lee Chiprout; Johanna Blom; Steven Long; John Weston—thank you for having the courage to join me on the front lines; Dr. Massouda Jalal (Jalal Foundation, Kabul); Brian Mayes; the members of the board of directors of OFWI and all the volunteers—without you none of this would be possible. I am not a hero but a man who is blessed to work with heroes. Thank you for your sacrifices of time, finances, energy, and sleep, and for standing for the truth no matter what.

ENDORSEMENTS

Majed El Shafie is a rare human being. Having survived extreme persecution and torture for his faith in Jesus, he has devoted his life to rescuing others who are also being persecuted for their faith, often putting his own life on the line to do so. What could be more Jesus-like? I admire his courage and find it enticingly contagious!

Sid Roth
Host, *It's Supernatural!* television program

With his film, Freedom Fighter, and now its subsequent book, Majed El Shafie has done another service to the many families and people around the world who are viciously persecuted because of their religious faith. By continuously drawing attention to these egregious violations of the most basic human rights, Freedom Fighter and other such works encourage greater involvement by Canadians and by governments throughout the free world in doing what we can to help those in need and to relieve their suffering.

Every man, woman, and child on earth has a fundamental right to freedom of conscience and religion. Those of us who are blessed to live in that freedom in countries like Canada must not close our eyes to the plight of our fellow man in countries of persecution. We must not forget their suffering, we must not overlook the crimes against them, and we must continue to pray for them and work for their safety and protection.

I am pleased to commend Freedom Fighter and the work of all who continue to fight for justice for the oppressed.

THE HONOURABLE JASON KENNEY
Minister of Citizenship, Immigration and Multiculturalism

Remember that the persecuted Christians are dying every day, but they are still smiling. They are in a deep, dark night, but they still have the candle of hope. The enemy may have a very strong weapon and a very strong army, but we have the Lord Almighty. They can kill the dreamer, but they cannot kill the dream.

CONTENTS

PREFACE

They can kill the dreamer, but they cannot kill the dream.

FREEDOM FIGHTER IS A TREATISE of the continuing and escalating abuse of Christians, Jews, and other religious minorities worldwide and highlights my work on behalf of the persecuted Church and other oppressed religious minorities through my organization, One Free World International. Traveling worldwide, I investigate claims of abuse, persecution, and slavery and take every opportunity to speak truth to governments that neglect and violate the human rights of their citizens.

From Egypt to China, Afghanistan to Pakistan, the true stories and indisputable statistics reveal the reality of people being silenced—killed, tortured, maimed—because of their religious beliefs. Especially poignant is my own imprisonment, death sentence, and eventual escape—but even more heartbreaking and horribly typical is the story of a 2½-year-old Pakistani girl who suffered violent sexual abuse because of her family's Christian beliefs. One Free World International worked for three years to rescue little Neha and her family—but there are countless more children and families who need help.

Many choose to dismiss this harsh reality—I choose to fight for one free world.

Article 18 of the *Universal Declaration of Human Rights*, declares that:

> Everyone has the right to freedom of thought, conscience and religion; this right includes freedom to change his religion or belief, and freedom, either alone or in community with others and in public or private, to manifest his religion or belief in teaching, practice, worship and observance.

Yet persecution of human beings because of their religion is a significant and underestimated problem—and Christians are the main targets. It is estimated that every three minutes somewhere in the world a Christian faces serious violations ranging from severe discrimination to outright persecution of their basic right to freedom of religion. Each year about 165,000 people are murdered simply because they are Christians. In total, between 200 million and 300 million Christians worldwide live with the constant threat of persecution because of their faith.

After the collapse of the Soviet Union, state-sponsored persecution of religion does not seem the formidable threat it once was. Yet communist countries like China (with about one-fifth of the world's population), North Korea, Vietnam, and Cuba continue to control and even outlaw religion in favor of atheist ideology. Many Muslim states discriminate, persecute, and outlaw all religions other than Islam.

But a more dangerous and worrisome trend is developing with the rise in religious extremism. Specifically, in some countries the government avoids responsibility by claiming to be a democracy and respect the human rights of its citizens—all the while permitting non-state actors, individuals or groups with various motivations, to attack and persecute religious minorities without consequences. This development in religious extremism and related impunity requires states assessing refugee claims to re-evaluate existing presumptions of state protection and the availability of internal relocation options. These doctrines are often relied on as grounds to deny refugee claims but, despite country information available to decision makers that often indicates otherwise, these options may not be available to those fleeing religious persecution under these circumstances.

I believe that respect for human rights should be one of the world's most valued priorities—and religious freedom is certainly one of the most basic human rights. As a result, religious persecution demands a response from governments worldwide through effective foreign policy and urgent reforms to refugee protection systems.

◄○►

In an article written by Teresa Neumann for *Breaking Christian News* titled "Persecuted Muslim Convert to Christianity Urges Love and Forgiveness," she begins with this Reporter's Note:

> I must confess, I've always been squeamish when it comes to stories of Christian persecution. I'd just as soon hear a one sentence synopsis from a third party—something like: "Pastor X was stoned to death for his faith in Jesus in Timbuktu, isn't that awful?"—than read, or worse yet see, the gory details written in journals or splashed across a huge movie screen. It's a bit too close for comfort.
>
> But then, I guess we're not called to comfort; sometimes we're called to sacrificial confrontation, and in that vein, there seems to be a change in the air. I can smell it when I see trailers for the soon-to-be-released

film, *The End of the Spear* and I smelled it again when I read this story of a Muslim Egyptian, who after he was saved, was willing to lay his life down for Christ. May we all remember that the Body of Christ (or the "dreamers" as this saint calls us) is composed of "Red, black, yellow, brown, and white—they are precious in His sight!"—Teresa Neumann, for *Breaking Christian News*.

A report in the *Finger Lake Times* out of Geneva, N.Y., showcases the astounding life of Muslim-turned Christian Majed El Shafie, whose "seven hellish days of torture in an Egyptian prison" ignited a passion for helping other persecuted Christians worldwide. Urging "love and forgiveness in the face of terrible hardship," El Shafie, founder of Toronto-based One Free World Ministries, is sharing his testimony to lawmakers in the U.S., Canada and Israel in the hopes of relieving the plight of persecuted Christians in Asia and the Middle East.

> "I decided to forgive those who tortured me, but with forgiveness comes action," he said. "We have to help the people that are suffering for their beliefs."

Reporter Mike Maslanik trails El Shafie's life, noting that he was born into a prominent Muslim family in Cairo. His father and brother are successful attorneys and an uncle serves as a judge on a high court.

> "When you're born into a family like this, you have lots of books on law, justice and freedom," he said. While studying law in Alexandria [Egypt], El Shafie was reportedly shocked to see the harsh treatment of Christians. Building churches is illegal in Egypt, he said, and Christians are treated worse than second-class citizens.

It was about this time that El Shafie began studying the Bible and in 1998, at about 20 years of age, he gave his life to Christ and organized an underground congregation—worshiping in caves—that attracted 24,000 worshipers within two years.

But trouble began in earnest when El Shafie appealed for equal rights for Christians. He was arrested and confined in Abu Jaabel prison in Cairo, a place locals call "Hell on Earth," charged with inciting a revolution, trying to change Egypt's religion to Christianity and "worshiping and loving Jesus Christ."

According to the report, while in custody, El Shafie refused to name names [of his friends and other Christians] so his captors took him to "an underground portion of the prison and tortured him for seven days straight," shaving his head and holding him under scalding hot then freezing cold water. When that didn't work, they hung him upside down, beating him with belts, burning him with cigarettes and tearing his toenails out. Finally, the prison guards tied him to a cross and left him there for two [and a half] days.

After losing consciousness, he found himself later waking up in a hospital bed. When a guard tipped him off that he was about to be executed, he escaped out of a back window, rode across the Red Sea on a jet ski, crossed the Sinai Desert and turned himself in to the Israeli government where he remained in custody for 16 months while the United Nations and Amnesty International investigated his story.

Ultimately, he was given political-refugee status and immigrated to Canada.

Becoming a Christian, notes Maslanik, cost El Shafie his home and his family, who have since disowned him, but he gained a new purpose in life as an advocate for persecuted Christians. "This whole thing changed my life," he said. "I'm not giving up because I know people are going through that."

To all governments that persecute Christians, El Shafie offers this message: "The persecuted Christians are dying, but they're still smiling. They're in a [dark night] , but they're holding the light of the Lord. You can kill the dreamer, but you can't kill the dream."[1]

INTRODUCTION

THIS BOOK TELLS A STORY. It is a true story, the story of hundreds of millions of people around the world today who are suffering because of what they believe and how they worship. At the same time, it is the story of what one person can do to bring hope and peace into the world if that person can count on the people around them to stand up, sacrifice some of their ease and comfort, and join the fight for truth and justice.

Join me on this journey as we travel to exotic lands bursting with sights and sounds that mystify and intrigue but where death and darkness rule behind a false façade of religion and respectability.

We will travel to Egypt, home of the pyramids and the Sphinx and the largest Christian community dating its continuous presence back to the time of Christ in the world. Yet after centuries of Islamic domination and decades of repression under an iron-fisted dictator, this community is now under threat to its very existence. The dictator is gone but when you witness the events that took place both on his authority and despite his repressive regime you will question with us what lies ahead as the extremists he barely kept in check are poised to take over the reins of power.

Pakistan will leave you speechless as we visit modern-day slave camps and speak with villagers who have recently been freed from such camps. We will walk through villages where Christian families live in unimaginable squalor, simply because they are Christians and therefore not accepted by the rest of society. You will learn about the blasphemy laws that require death on conviction and how they are used mostly to settle personal vendettas or to try to blackmail minorities into converting to Islam. The unwavering support of this country by the West will baffle you.

The twin official religions of communist China are atheism and secular materialism. Some of you will argue that atheism is not a religion, but the semantics are trivial. Atheism at its very core is based on a belief about God, even if that belief is that God does not exist, and in countries like Egypt and Pakistan atheists are persecuted precisely because they deny God. But in China, on the other hand, atheists rule and those who do not subscribe or conform to the accepted, sanitized, and controlled religious teachings authorized by the government are pushed to the margins of society where they are harassed and imprisoned while the rest of society pursues its worship of money and material wealth.

Join with us as we are taken to visit labor camps where religious dissenters are forced to manufacture export products that perhaps you purchase, not thinking twice about where they come from, just excited you got a good deal... Further down the corridor other religious dissenters are being killed to provide high quality organs on demand for transplant to wealthy, western patients who ask no questions. And in the meantime, the government controls all information so that those inside and outside have no idea of what is really happening behind the bamboo curtain.

From China we will journey on to Iraq where the Christian population that has existed there for almost two thousand years, since shortly after the time of Christ, has been reduced to half its size in less than ten years. Iraqi Christians have been killed or forced to leave their homeland for their own safety as a result of kidnappings, demands to convert to Islam accompanied by threats, and attacks on their churches. Sabean Mandaeans, a curious group almost exclusive to Iraq whose history dates back possibly to around the time of Christ or earlier, are faced with the same threats and are now only 10 percent of the community they were just ten years ago. Yet our governments steadfastly refuse to affirm that genocides are taking place in this country.

Finally, we will travel to Afghanistan, a country where ninety-nine percent of the population are Muslims. There are very small historic communities of Sikhs and Hindus, among others, but the only Christians are those few who have converted from Islam. This tiny community of 500 to 8,000 converts must worship in secret because if their conversion becomes known they will be killed. They may be killed by their families or communities, but in this country where so many of our young men and women have died over the last ten years fighting for freedom and human rights, the greatest threat these secret Christians face is being found out by their new, western-backed government which has undertaken an official campaign to root out and kill converts. And in a country where the deterioration of women's rights or even gay rights can be discussed openly with authorities, the one group that has no rights about which to even begin a discussion is the Christian converts.

As you begin to process the reality that these things are actually taking place in our world today—these events are not some medieval inquisition or Orwellian science fiction story but the reality of the twenty-first century—we will take you to meet people like Magdi Yousef whose bookstore north of Cairo was destroyed when one of his employees converted to Christianity. Magdi was accused of converting him and selling books that attack Islam and for this he was attacked by religious extremists and detained and tortured by authorities. He sought safety by claiming refugee status in Canada but Canadian authorities refused to believe him and sent him back to Egypt to be tortured again.

We will ride together into darkness and danger in Pakistan as we rescue little Neha whose family has lived in hiding for four years after Neha was kidnapped and raped for the simple reason that her father would not convert to Islam. She was two years old…

You will sit by the bedside of Attra, a young Christian man from Iraq who is now paralyzed, as he tells you how he was kidnapped and tortured by his fellow countrymen. When Attra refused to convert to Islam or kill an American soldier and could not pay the $250,000 ransom demanded, his kidnappers shot him in the back and left him for dead on the side of the road.

We will take you to Gojra, a small town in Pakistan where one summer evening in 2009 thousands of Muslims from the surrounding areas attacked the local Christians, burned their homes, and even barricaded a family in their blazing home burning them alive. Police heard the threats issued openly from mosques the day before but stood by and did nothing to stop the mob. Instead they set up roadblocks the only impact of which was to prevent fire crews from accessing the scene.

As we visit Yad Vashem in Jerusalem we will talk about anti-semitism and how, a mere generation after the holocaust, this murderous hatred is once again on the rise in unexpected quarters. We will discuss how this should be of great concern to us, whether or not we are Jews, as hatred only breeds more hate and antisemitism is the harbinger of broader atrocities.

Along our journey through some of the darkest places on the planet we will show you that, while persecution of those who are different is clearly wrong, the real problem is not the persecution, but the silence… It is the deafening silence that falls over us as the screams of tortured and dying Christians, Falun Gong members, Bahá'í's, Hindus, dissident or non-mainstream Muslims, and others echo in the ears of the West…

Before you descend into despair, however, we will introduce you to some of the people who have heard the echoes and have decided to do something about it. You will meet Chantal Desloges, a Toronto immigration lawyer who gives tirelessly of her time and energy to help secure effective solutions for refugees. You will meet the Honourable Jason Kenney, Canadian Minister of Citizenship and Immigration and indefatigable advocate for human rights. Mario Silva, who as a member of parliament and despite the dangers took on the challenge to join us to see for himself firsthand what is happening in some of these countries, will share his impressions. You will also get to know Sharon Harel, an Israeli human rights advocate who will share ways that you can get involved.

You will join us as we meet with government leaders in Afghanistan and Pakistan and confront them with the abuses taking place in their countries and with their governments' responsibility. Back home in the West you will walk the halls of power with us as we testify before government committees to educate decision makers about the atrocities that are being committed against religious minorities around the world today.

Finally, we will talk about ways that you can become freedom fighters alongside us. Our fight is not a war with guns, tanks, or missiles nor does it require specialized military training. Our weapons are words, ideas, your keyboard, and the internet and anyone concerned about truth and justice can enlist. Your rules of engagement consist of actions like informing yourself of what is happening; participating in letter-writing campaigns, demonstrations, and boycotts; supporting organizations like OFWI that are on the front lines with your prayers and financial support; sponsoring refugees; voting for candidates who are willing to speak the truth and do something about these issues; and sharing what is going on with your friends and family and people whom you meet in your day-to-day routine.

So, are you ready? Join with us as we continue the fight…

1

A LITTLE BACKGROUND

"If I tell you about my faith, it will change our friendship forever," my best friend Tamir said. But I pressured him—and then I trusted him when he gave me a Bible and told me I would find all the answers I needed in its pages. I studied this book carefully in the days and weeks to come and little by little, although it was dangerous to turn my back on Islam—the faith of my family for generations, the love of Christ began to open my heart and fill my spirit.

ALTHOUGH THIS BOOK IS NOT about me, I was convinced by others close to me that it would be helpful if you knew a bit about me and why I feel an obligation to write this book—for all those who are suffering worldwide because of their beliefs.

I was born in Cairo, Egypt, into a prominent Muslim family of lawyers; and following in the footsteps of my father and uncles, I chose to become a lawyer as well.

But through the witness of my best friend, Tamir, I experienced the love of Christ and gave my life and service to the Lord. I began a ministry in Egypt to bring the Christian community all of the same legal rights that the Muslim community had always enjoyed. In just two years, the ministry grew to include 24,000

Christians. Although it is illegal to build churches, the ministry built two churches inside the nearby mountains; also, a Bible school and a medical clinic were built to tend to the spiritual and physical needs of the oppressed Christians. I also established a newspaper in which I regularly requested from the Egyptian government the same equal rights for the Christian community.

The Egyptian government did not tolerate my outspokenness and work on behalf of the Christians; and after the second church was built, at the age of 21, I was arrested and sent to Abu Zaabel prison—a place I can best describe as hell on earth—in Cairo, Egypt's capital city.

During my time in prison, I suffered severe torture from guards who always wore masks and referred to each other by numbers rather than names. As mentioned in the article quoted in the Preface, for seven days in the underground prison I experienced everything from being stripped naked and remaining that way day after day to having my head shaved and having steaming hot and then bitter cold water poured over me. My toenail was torn out causing excruciating pain, and I was hung upside down and burned over and over again with hot, lit cigarettes.

However, in the midst of the pain and darkness, when all I could smell and taste was sweat and blood, I experienced a miracle! When three large, vicious guard dogs were commanded to attack me, they went silent and didn't lunge toward me with their sharp and bared teeth. I praised God for this miracle and thanked Him for His mercy.

During the last two and a half days in the torture chamber, I was "crucified"—my hands and feet tied tightly to a wooden cross. With a long, curved, sharp knife, my bare back was sliced open in several places. Then a mixture of salt and lemon was poured into the open, bleeding wounds. The pain was excruciating; I wished to die.

Passing out from the unbearable pain, I woke up in a hospital and eventually escaped through a whirlwind journey, fleeing to Israel, where I was jailed for over a year because the Israeli government did not know what to do with me under the circumstances. Legally I could not stay in Israel, but if I was sent back to Egypt, I would have been executed—this I knew for certain.

All of the cruel torture and subsequent death sentence was because I wouldn't reveal the names of other Christians—all because of my new faith in the Lord Jesus Christ.

Through the intervention of Amnesty International, the United Nations, and the International Christian Embassy Jerusalem, I eventually obtained political asylum in Canada and became a citizen in 2006.

I have visited and spoken in hundreds of churches and congregations in both Canada and the United States to bring awareness to Christians who may not know the barbaric reality of their brothers' and sisters' lives in other parts of the world. I have also been interviewed for magazine articles and on television and radio programs—both Christian and secular—all in an effort to aid those who are suffering, those who have no voice beyond their silent screams for help.

My passion is to alleviate the pain of all those being persecuted worldwide because of their religion. My story is not only a story of violence and persecution but a story of glory and victory. It's a story about fighting the darkness with the light of Christ.

The remainder of the book shares with you modern-day, real-life stories of people suffering for their beliefs. Also, there are histories and current events presented that highlight the intolerance and violence perpetrated against people worldwide in countries that ignore common human rights and decency. I must expose these acts against humanity in hopes of bringing awareness to these acts and encouraging and motivating others to do what they can to help.

At the beginning of each chapter, I continue my story of religious persecution and I conclude each chapter with Neha's story—the young Pakistani child who was violently raped because her father, her family, would not convert to Islam.

Work for Christians is hard to come by in Pakistan. Neha and her parents and siblings lived together in the countryside where the children played together. Neha's father finally found work on a farm and the family felt secure—until the landowner for whom he worked began to daily pressure him to convert to Islam. He firmly refused.

2

EGYPT

I was working late at night when the knock came at my door, crisp and official... The officers took me to Abu Zaabel prison in Cairo where I was now in a small, filthy cell deep underground thinking about Tamir. "I have to keep going. I can't let Tamir's death be for nothing." When he had pushed me out of the way and the bullet had hit him instead of me, as the blood was flowing from his heart and his young life was slipping away, I will never forget his last words as I held him in my arms, "Continue the fight..." Until today, every morning I wake up to honor his last request and my solemn promise, and his memory gave me strength in those dark, frightening, and lonely hours.

WHILE GROWING UP IN EGYPT, never in my first 19 years did it enter my mind that there were terrible atrocities being committed against people throughout the country because of their beliefs. Despite Egypt's appearance as a democracy, it has, in fact, been ruled for decades as a dictatorship by successive presidents. The only recognized religions are Islam, Christianity, and Judaism (which is nearly nonexistent). This means that all other religions, particularly Baha'is are not even acknowledged and definitely not accepted.

Islam is the dominant and official religion, and Islamic fundamentalism is a powerful force. Under the constitution, Islamic sharia law is the basis for all legislation—and any religious practices that conflict with sharia law are prohibited. Sharia is the entire body of Islamic law. It is a wide-ranging body of law and personal rules, regulating matters of jurisprudence, hygiene, politics, business, banking, family, sexuality, diet, and society.

Members of religious minorities experience serious violations of their rights on a daily basis, ranging from discrimination in official matters, for example employment, to intimidation, threats, and physical violence against property and the person—including death.

Police and security forces do not come to the assistance of religious minorities and often charge the victims when they try to register a complaint. When confronted by security forces, members of religious minorities face the possibility of torture—confirmed by international observers as a systemic problem in Egypt.

HUMAN RIGHTS IN EGYPT

Egypt is a predominately Muslim country with a population of approximately 77 million. The history of Christianity in Egypt dates to the Roman era. Alexandria was an early center of Christianity, and from the 4th century until the Islamic conquest of Egypt in the 7th century, Egypt was predominantly Christian. Nevertheless, Christians today account for only approximately 10 percent of the population and do not enjoy the same rights as Muslims. Specifically, their freedom of worship is limited and they face daily restrictions on their rights—solely because they are Christians. For example, building churches is not permitted. Even making simple repairs to an existing church requires special governmental permission, although both mosques and bars can be built freely. Even though Christianity is recognized by the government, Christians are treated as second-class citizens in every respect and left at the mercy of Islamic fundamentalists.

Those belonging to unrecognized religions, like the approximately 2,000 who practice the Baha'i religion, are unable to obtain identity cards and are essentially legal nonpersons. The government's policy in this respect was affirmed in December 2006 when the Supreme Administrative Court decided the case of a Baha'i couple, Husam Izzat Musa and Ranya Enayat Rushdy. A lower court had ordered the government to issue the couple identity cards that properly identified their religion. The state appealed and the Supreme Administrative Court overturned the decision, affirming the government's policy that only the three recognized religions could be stated on identity cards. Without identity cards, Baha'is are unable to obtain an education, own property, or engage in numerous routine matters of citizenship and daily life. Muslim converts to Christianity face many of the same problems and have been charged with falsifying documents for obtaining Christian identity papers.

MUSLIM BROTHERHOOD

Converts are also faced with the threat of death for apostasy from Islamic fundamentalists.

Islamic fundamentalism is very strong in Egypt. For example, the Muslim Brotherhood was founded in Egypt in 1928, "with the goal of spreading Islamic Sharia law worldwide and uniting all Muslim nations into one Islamic super state." The Muslim Brotherhood "was eventually banned in Egypt, but for the past several decades has worked behind the scenes to the point where it is now considered the most influential Islamist organization in the world—with chapters in more than 100 countries. Before Osama bin Laden formed al Qaeda, he belonged to the Muslim Brotherhood. So did his top deputy, Ayman al-Zawahiri and the 9/11 mastermind Khalid Sheikh Mohammed. In addition, the terrorist group Hamas identifies itself as the Muslim Brother-hood's Palestinian branch."[1]

In January 2012, Egypt's Muslim Brotherhood's political party, the Freedom and Justice Party, won the largest number of parliamentary seats in the first election after President Hosni Murbarak was ousted in a "popular" uprising in April 2011. The Muslim Brotherhood is known for its violent and discriminating posture on anything or anyone non-Muslim and we will discuss the divergence between its rhetoric in the current political climate and its stated goals a little later in this chapter.

Extremists have penetrated many government agencies and can now, after the 2012 election results, openly exercise influence over government action—or inaction in many cases. As President Mubarak was known to simply pay lip-service to human rights conventions and international conferences for the protection of religious freedom and human rights, the reality now will be even more devastating for many of Egypt's citizenry.

There are, at any given time, 6,000-7,000 Christians in prison in Egypt for the simple fact that they are Christians. In October 2003, the Egyptian government released around 1,000 members of the Islamist fundamentalist group Gammaa el-Islamiya, which was responsible for the bombing of tourists in Luxor in 1997 and other terrorist activities. At the very same time the government was pursuing a campaign to detain and torture Christians who had converted from Islam. Approximately 20 converts were charged with falsifying identity papers because they had obtained identity papers bearing new, Christian names.

Despite the restrictions on their rights, life is tolerable for most Egyptian Christians as long as they maintain a low profile and bear their circumstances in silence; however, they must constantly be on their guard against any real or perceived offense to their Muslim neighbors, which can result in everything from simple harassment and property damage—to torture and death of the perceived offender(s) or their family members. Christian girls also face the danger of kidnapping and forced marriage to Muslim men and related forced conversion.

While government agencies are sometimes directly involved either officially or unofficially, the perpetrators most often are family members, neighbors, friends, employers, or local mobs, often with the tacit approval or encouragement of the police or other government agencies.

The offense that can bring on the wrath of the Muslim community, leaving Christians with no option but to flee, can be as simple as: dating a Muslim, explaining Christianity to a Muslim, helping a Muslim convert to Christianity, assisting a Christian who had been forced to convert to Islam, or simply refusing to convert to Islam when invited or pressured to do so. And the offense serving as pretext for an attack can be based on allegations, suggestions, rumor, a misinterpretation of the facts, or even an unrelated personal dispute.

Under these circumstances, once a Christian has attracted the attention of Muslim fundamentalists, even through what could be inadvertent action on their part or the simple exercise of their right to freedom of religion, they are marked in society and cannot escape the threats and persecution wherever they go. If the government security services have been involved in the incident, the unfortunate Christian will likely be placed on an internal watch list.

In addition, Egyptian society is not closed like North American society—there is no privacy. When a newcomer arrives in a community or neighborhood, people probe the newcomer's background and private affairs with great interest, and it does not take long for details about the person's past and identity to be known. Moreover, Christians stand out even more in a new community and therefore attract special attention. Thus even if the authorities do not get involved, local Islamic extremists will pursue any

Christians found to have been caught in any issues with Muslims in the past.

FALSELY ACCUSED

Magdi Yousef, an Egyptian Christian, lived in peace for a number of years—until he was falsely accused of trying to convert a Muslim to Christianity. "They burned my shop and smashed my car—then they chased me," Magdi said with tears in his eyes. He feared for his life and fled to Canada, but the government there rejected him because the official charged with determining his case did not believe that such persecution could happen in a country such as Egypt. He was returned to Egypt where he was immediately taken into custody and tortured. They stripped him naked and beat him with a rope. The men who beat him and burned him with lit cigarettes mocked him, saying that they were "decorating his back like the back of Jesus." He felt as if he had no hope. After being released and feeling even more threatened, Magdi contacted One Free World International and through diplomatic communications and providing evidence, Magdi was rescued and lives and worships freely in Canada.

Most threatening incidents happen out of the public eye. We do not hear about them in North America and they certainly do not make the evening news. They can involve anything from property damage to physical violence and threats (including death threats), usually by private individuals, or harassment or torture by state security agencies. Christians are afraid to report the events because even if the police were to assist them, which is usually not the case, they are afraid of bringing additional threats and violence against themselves or their families because they have reported the incident.

Nevertheless, occasionally a case is too significant to escape the notice of the public, even as far away as North America.

The El-Kosheh massacre involved the killing of 21 Christians and the destruction of hundreds of Christian homes and businesses by a Muslim mob provoked by an argument between a Muslim and a Christian shop owner in December 1999. The police and security forces either stood by or actively participated in the violence. No one was ever found guilty of the deaths of the Christians.

This event was preceded by an incident in 1998 when more than 1,000 Christians had been detained and tortured by police in the course of a murder investigation into the deaths of two local Christians in an attempt to pin the murders, widely believed to have been committed by Muslims, on a Christian. These events are typical of how often the Christian victims themselves are arrested and tortured in response to persecution by their Muslim neighbors. Moreover, they were widely perceived to indicate a green light on the part of the authorities for local Muslims to murder and harass Christians.

In October 2005, a mob attempted to destroy a church in Alexandria because two years earlier it had presented a single performance of a play depicting the life of a Christian who converts to Islam and then tries to convert back to Christianity. The state security forces protected the church, but over the course of several days a nun was stabbed, threats were made against Christian priests, and several other churches in Alexandria were attacked and damaged resulting in parishioners being afraid to attend Sunday worship. In addition to property damage, on one day about 90 people were injured, including 20 police officers, and four died (two police officers and two demonstrators) during the violence.

During pre-Easter celebrations in April 2006, three men armed with knives entered three Alexandria area churches in what appeared to have been coordinated attacks. The attackers killed one and wounded at least 12 people. Police provided security for the churches, but reportedly stood by without taking any action to protect the worshipers. Moreover, as they typically do, authorities minimized the attacks and downplayed their religious implications by arresting one individual and alleging his actions were due to mental illness. Clashes erupted the next day between Christians taking part in a funeral ceremony for the victim and police who disrupted the funeral procession.

JEWS IN EGYPT

The Jewish community in Egypt is virtually nonexistent, an estimated 100-200 elderly individuals. Despite the peace agreement between Israel and Egypt that is in force and prohibits "hostile propaganda," anti-Semitism continues and is on the increase in both official and nonofficial forums. Government-run and opposition media regularly run anti-Semitic cartoons, articles, and television programs that demonize Jews and Israel or deny the Holocaust. Jews and Israelis are presented through derogatory and racist stereotypes—as Nazis and cold-blooded killers, or as conspirators controlling the American government or seeking to control the world. School textbooks ignore the existence of Israel and give students a distorted view of Israel, Judaism, and Christianity. In the wake of the overthrow of Mubarak's regime, leading members of the Islamic parties that have risen to prominence have made it clear that they do not intend to live up to the commitments in the peace agreement with Israel. How they will act on those statements is only a matter of time.

[handwritten margin note: Egypt had a large and ancient Jewish community, but it was ethnically cleansed in the last 100 years. Many young Egyptians don't know that Jews lived there until a few generations ago.]

WORLDWIDE FOREIGN POLICY AND EGYPT

One Free World International believes that countries in the free world must not be afraid to use all means at their disposal to make a stand for what is right. In particular, Western countries must take a strong stand with regard to religious freedom throughout the world and particularly in countries like Egypt. Specifically, governments in these countries must:

- use their diplomatic and other relations with Egypt, from aid and trade relations to training and educational or cultural exchanges, etc., to promote religious freedom.

- confront Egypt with their failures both directly and in international forums.

- downgrade their relationship with Egypt, reducing trade, aid, investment, and diplomatic cooperation when it does not respond positively to other measures.

I believe that especially nations based on Christian traditions and values must stand on principle and not worry about the immediate political or diplomatic consequences. History will not judge us on whether we gained or lost a trade treaty in the short term. History will judge us on what we contributed to the long-term improvement of the human condition on this planet.

Great strides can be made if we promote religious freedom through diplomacy, but where such efforts are unsuccessful, aid and trade relationships provide a practical but peaceful means to demonstrate the importance of these issues to authorities in countries such as Egypt. For example, Canada's relationship with Egypt is very good and includes a trade relationship of almost $1.2 billion (2011) in two-way trade[2] and aid in the amount of almost $18 million annually,[3] according to the Department of Foreign Affairs and the Canadian International Development Agency. Canada must use this relationship to promote religious freedom and to confront Egypt for its systematic violations of human rights and for allowing Islamist groups to operate against religious minorities with impunity. The government must speak out and demand that Egypt live up to international human rights standards and, in particular, its own stated commitments to international human rights. If it fails to do so, the Canadian and American governments must be prepared to scale back aid, trade, and cultural programs in order to deliver a clear message to Egyptian authorities that such cooperation will only be available if Egypt makes credible efforts to meet its human rights obligations to its own people.

According to the U.S. Department of State website, security and economic assistance to Egypt expanded significantly in the wake of the Egyptian-Israeli Peace Treaty in 1979. U.S. military aid to Egypt totals over $1.3 billion annually. And in addition, the U.S. Agency for International Development (USAID) has provided over $28 billion in economic and development assistance to Egypt since 1975. Early assistance focused on infrastructure, health, food supply, and agriculture. The Commodity Import Program, through which USAID provided hundreds of millions of dollars in financing to enable the Egyptian private sector to import U.S. goods between 1986 and 2008, was one of the largest and most popular USAID programs. Current programs focus on trade and investment; utilities; education; healthier, planned families; natural resources; democracy and governance; and other programs supported by the Middle East Partnership Initiative.[4] The avenues to communicate with Egyptian authorities on these issues are numerous.

Beyond its general obligations to international standards recognized in the Universal Declaration of Human Rights, Egypt has specific obligations under international law. It has signed and ratified both the International Covenant on Civil and Political Rights (ICCPR) and the International Covenant on Economic, Social and Cultural Rights. When signing these covenants, Egypt undertook to respect and ensure all rights recognized in the documents to all individuals within its territory and jurisdiction, without distinction as to religion.

Moreover, Article 18 of the ICCPR states specifically:

1. Everyone shall have the right to freedom of thought, conscience and religion. This right shall include freedom to have or to adopt a religion or belief of his choice, and freedom, either individually or in community

with others and in public or private, to manifest his religion or belief in worship, observance, practice and teaching.

2. No one shall be subject to coercion which would impair his freedom to have or to adopt a religion or belief of his choice.

Yet the Egyptian government does not recognize all religions or ensure its citizens' freedom to choose and practice the religion of their choice nor does it provide equal protection to all its citizens. By failing to provide for the equal rights of all its citizens, even in matters as basic as the issuing of identity cards which would enable minority citizens to exercise the rights and freedoms guaranteed in these documents, the Egyptian government is in clear violation of its international obligations and commitments. In order to show that they are serious about human rights in Egypt and to reinforce their message to the Egyptian government, Western nations founded on Christian principles especially must not keep this a private matter to be dealt with informally in bilateral relations. Canada and other morally conscious countries must confront Egypt about its failures in multilateral forums such as the United Nations.

Egypt has the largest population in the Middle East and promotes itself as a democracy even though it has been run like a dictatorship by successive presidents, including the ousted President Hosni Mubarak. Nevertheless, religious minorities, particularly Christians, continue to live a second-class existence in constant fear of being targeted for violence and not having any recourse simply because of their religion. Magdi Yousef, I, and many thousands of others can attest to this fact of Egyptian life.

Our governments must not continue to trade with or provide aid to Egypt or cooperate with it on a diplomatic, military, or cultural level unless and until Egypt improves its treatment of religious minorities so that it meets international human rights standards in this area both in law and in the practical reality faced by its citizens in their daily lives.

THE DESIRE TO BELIEVE

Freedom of religion is one of the most fundamental human rights. The ability to believe or not to believe in something beyond our material existence in accordance with our individual conscience, and to manifest that belief in practices and observances, is one of the distinguishing characteristics of humanity. Persecution of people for their beliefs or coercing others into adopting certain beliefs denies the very humanity of the person who is thus violated.

If countries like the United States, Canada, and Great Britain wish to take seriously their commitment to human rights both at home and abroad, they must take seriously the right to religious freedom and the issue of persecution of religious minorities. In this regard, they must begin by confronting Egypt with its failing record in this matter. If Egypt wishes to present itself in the international community as a democracy, it must live up to the international standards required of a democracy and guarantee the equal rights of its citizens in fact and not just on paper. We must not be satisfied with any less.

JANUARY 1, 2011

As we in the West rejoiced and celebrated the birth of Christ in peace and plenty, attended Christmas services and feasted with friends and family, our brothers and sisters around the world were under attack as they tried to share in the celebrations.

On New Year's Eve, in the early hours of January 1, 2011, at least 21 were killed and more than 70 injured in Egypt when a bomb exploded outside the al-Qiddissin Coptic church in Alexandria where approximately 1,000 people had gathered to celebrate a New Year's mass. The mass was coming to a close and worshipers were beginning to leave the church when the bomb, loaded with shrapnel for maximum carnage, exploded. Security was entirely inadequate and our OFWI sources in Egypt indicated that in the aftermath of the attack there were further attacks against victims in the hospital and that even the authorities attacked Coptic demonstrators.

This was the most serious single attack against Egypt's Coptic community in many years and Egypt's then President Hosni Mubarak condemned the attack, blaming foreign elements and characterizing it as an attack against all of Egypt. While his condemnation was welcome, his statement was a transparent attempt to avoid the responsibility of Egyptian authorities. We must not forget that such attacks are not uncommon in Egypt where Muslim extremism has deep roots and is gaining in strength and that the Egyptian government was on notice of potential attacks by organizations that had threatened precisely such actions.

Only one year previous, January 2010, a similar, though less sophisticated, attack took place against worshipers leaving a Coptic Christmas Eve celebration. Moreover, it was well-known that Al Qaeda-linked terrorist groups had made threats against Egyptian churches in the weeks leading up to the 2010 Christmas season. With this history of attacks and open threats, the origin of the attackers at Al-Qiddisin Church is of little importance and what matters is the dismal failure of Egyptian authorities to prevent the attack.

International leaders including the Pope Benedict XVI, United States President Barack Obama, and Canadian Foreign Affairs Minister Lawrence Cannon also condemned the attack. President Obama called it a "barbaric and heinous act" that was "clearly targeting Christian worshipers." Minister Cannon called it a "vicious attack" and called on "Egyptians of all faiths to work together to end sectarian violence." While we appreciate their concern, their comments reveal a serious lack of understanding of the issues that can only prevent any meaningful resolution.

Clearly this despicable event was another example of an intentional campaign by Muslim extremists and their sympathizers to attack Christians and other minority communities. Unless the Canadian, United States, and other governments recognize these attacks for what they are and respond appropriately, holding those responsible to account rather than apportioning blame to the victims through "politically correct" appeals to all sides, the extremists will freely continue their murderous attacks on defenseless minorities while the Egyptian government turns a blind eye and makes hollow statements for appearances.

FEBRUARY 2011—THE ARAB SPRING UPRISING

In February, I was interviewed by Rhonda Spivak, writing for *The Jerusalem Post*.[5] At that time, I had about 24,000 people in Egypt alone updating me about what was happening in Egypt during the "Arab Spring" uprising. I told the reporter that the Muslim Brotherhood used the demonstrations in Egypt to advance its agenda. "They are going street to street, door to door asking people to go out to demonstrate...They want a hand in the new government. They are being more aggressive, more active, and are coming out in full power." The Muslim Brotherhood is popular with the poor, illiterate people of Egypt "because they provide the basic food and necessities to them...The Muslim Brotherhood is very wealthy. They own supermarkets in Egypt and they get funds from countries such as Iran and Saudi Arabia."

The claim that the Muslim Brotherhood is a conservative, nonviolent movement could not be further from the truth. While it officially renounces violence, the Muslim Brotherhood is the ideological parent of terrorist movements such as Hamas and al-Qaida. Members and supporters of the Muslim Brotherhood are behind daily forced conversion attempts, violent attacks, and torture against Egyptian Christians. The Brotherhood cooperates with Hamas in Gaza and its leaders are determined to launch war against Israel.

This is a very serious matter and we cannot, under any circumstances, allow the Muslim Brotherhood to increase or solidify its influence in Egypt. To do so would be to condemn the Egyptian people, from Christians and other religious minorities to moderate and secular Muslims, to a regime of oppression and religious tyranny that will make Mubarak's repressive regime seem like a beacon of freedom.

I stated in the midst of the Egyptian uprising that I believe that if the Muslim Brotherhood rises to full power, they will declare at the outset that they respect the treaty with Israel, but shortly afterward they will want to reform the agreement. As I mentioned previously, this scenario has begun to play out slowly and surely before our very eyes. The people of Egypt have been living in darkness under a dictatorship for 30 years—they will not be able to adjust to the light right away. Thirty percent of the population is illiterate—they cannot read and write their own name.

True democracy will not happen in the beginning, because it is easier for uneducated masses to turn to extremism. Egypt needs slow change. Democracy as we know it in the West cannot simply be transplanted into Egypt, a country that has *never experienced any form of true democracy*. Democracy cannot survive where people cannot read their own constitution. It must be taught, nurtured, and brought to maturity so that it can flourish.

I am concerned that if democracy is brought to Egypt too quickly, we will see the same scenario that we saw in Gaza and the West Bank in 2006, where Hamas won the elections, or we risk repeating the Iranian scenario, where pro-democracy forces deposed the shah in 1979 but were quickly overcome by the radical Islamic ayatollahs.

When Egypt had elections in 2005, even though they were rigged, the (illegal) Muslim Brotherhood won 88 out of 454 seats in the Egyptian parliament. In reality, the Brotherhood obtained more than 88 seats; but once they got 88 seats, the regime shut down the elections completely. Clearly this was not democracy in action, but neither is a state where the people elect extremist parties because they have not been educated about democracy, equality, and human rights of minorities.

Egypt's peace treaty with Israel was not one that was really between people. It was a cold peace that the Egyptians entered into to secure money from the Americans. There is no love lost between Egypt and Israel. Mubarak's regime was supporting Hamas under the table by enabling the smuggling of weapons from Sinai into Gaza. There is now a large, well-equipped army in Egypt—due to American support Egypt received after entering into the peace agreement with Israel. It is a built-up modern and sophisticated army that could in the not-so-distant future be at war with Israel.

Unlike Egypt, the Arab gulf states are stable, even though there is no democracy there because the people are wealthy. Saudi Arabia has a higher standard of living than Egypt. In Egypt, due to Mubarak's corrupt regime, the rich have gotten richer and the poor have gotten poorer, and the middle class is disappearing. The average Egyptian salary is under $2 a day.

MASS EXODUS

At the end of 2011, Egypt's "Arab Spring" led to a mass exodus of the Coptic Christian community—Canada was their preferred destination. According to an opinion piece in *The Globe and Mail* by Lawrence Solomon on October 18, 2011:

> We've [Canada] received about a sixth of the 100,000 who have fled Egypt in the past six months amid persecution by Islamic fundamentalists.

> If history repeats itself, those numbers could become much larger—Egypt has 10 million to 18 million Copts and other Christians, the largest remaining Christian

population in the Middle East by far. Should their persecution continue, the great majority could well flee in what would amount to one of history's greatest forced emigrations.

Egypt's Arab Spring is unfolding exactly as Copts feared. Hosni Mubarak, though seen as an unvarnished dictator in the West, was a protector to the Copts. He not only allowed them previously denied religious freedoms—everything from the right to repair their churches to live broadcasts of Easter services—but he also punished Islamists who persecuted them.

In the wave of unrest unleashed by the Arab Spring, that protection is now gone. Flagrant Copt-killing began with a church bombing during a New Year's Eve mass that left more than 20 dead and dozens wounded, followed by another deadly attack during the Coptic Christmas on Jan. 7.

Islamists have been ratcheting up their incitement against Copts, calling them infidels and accusing them of being Western spies and traitors who are stockpiling arms in plots to secede from the country. This week, more than 20 Copts were killed in clashes with the army during a demonstration over an attack on a church.

As a result of their growing vulnerability, Christians are sorrowfully abandoning their homeland of almost 2,000 years. (Before the Arab invasion of the 7th century, Egypt was majority Christian.) "Copts are not emigrating abroad voluntarily, they are coerced into that by threats and intimidation," said Naguib Gabriel, director of the Cairo-based Egyptian Union of Human Rights Organizations. "If emigration of Christians, who constitute nearly 16 per cent of the Egyptian population, continues at the present rate, it

[handwritten margin notes:] wow. The Egyptian Jewish community faced similar false accusations and attacks. Similar things happened to ancient Jewish communities in other Middle Eastern and North African countries

may reach 250,000 by the end of 2011 and, within 10 years, a third of the Coptic population of Egypt would be gone."

This decline would follow the pattern of religious cleansing that characterizes much of the Middle East, which, in the 20th century, retained sizable Christian minorities in many countries and, in Lebanon, a majority. Lebanon's Christian majority is now reduced to about a third of its population, Syria's 33 percent is now down to 10 per cent, Turkey's 15 per cent is down to 1 per cent, Iran's is at 0.4 per cent, and Gaza's is at 0.2 per cent.

The loss of Egypt's Copts would obviously be a personal tragedy for the millions who'd be uprooted, but also a tragedy for those Egyptians remaining behind. The Copts form much of Egypt's professional and business class, and the loss of their expertise could cripple the country's already faltering economy. The only good to come would be found in the countries to which this talented community is emigrating—chiefly Canada, the United States, and various European countries.[6]

"DEMOCRATIC REVOLUTION" THREATENS CHRISTIANS IN EGYPT

The international media has moved on from Egypt as President Mubarak stepped down with reporters and analysts generally portraying these developments as a triumph for democracy and moderate Islam. On the ground, however, the situation is not nearly so clear-cut.

There were numerous attacks against Christians and Christian institutions in the weeks following the revolts, and since the Egyptian army assumed control from President Mubarak. In fact, attacks against two monasteries on February 23, 2011, were both carried out by the army itself. It used small arms, heavy machine guns, and armored personnel carriers to destroy protective walls around the monasteries and attack the inhabitants. At the Anba Bishoy monastery, one monk and six church workers were shot and wounded; and at the Anba Makarious Al Sakandarie Monastery, soldiers broke into the monastery and beat some of the Christians in the compound. These attacks were intended to harass and threaten the Christian community, using as an excuse the claim that the monasteries did not have permits for the walls that had been built to protect against raiders and criminals.

Other attacks have been carried out by civilians. On March 4, 2011, a Muslim mob looted a local church in Sool, a town south of Cairo, desecrated remains found in the church, and burned it down almost killing a priest in the process. The mob had been motivated by a local imam who had called for congregants to "kill all the Christians," stating that they had "no right" to live in the area. When the fire died down the next day, the mob destroyed the remainder of the church and offered Islamic prayers on the ruins, pledging to build a mosque on the site. Others blockaded the village vowing to turn it into a Muslim town. Many Christians fled, but women who remained in the area reported that they were sexually assaulted.

Thousands of Christians demonstrated in Cairo in the days following the Sool attack, demanding protection and recognition of the persecution. On March 9, 2011 the protests turned violent as a Muslim mob attacked the Christian demonstrators. Thirteen Christians died and 140 were wounded in the ensuing violence as security forces and the army stood by and watched.

Lara Logan is an American journalist. While covering the Egyptian uprisings in Cairo's Tahrir Square in February 2011, she was surrounded by an angry mob of men, pulled away from the television crew she was working with, and brutally sexually abused. This savage attack happened to a foreigner in Egypt, an American with the might of the most powerful country in the world behind her. If a mob in the midst of a demonstration ostensibly clamoring for democracy would do this to her, how much more vulnerable are Egyptian citizens. How much more would a frenzied mob of Islamic extremists and uneducated Muslims incited by their imams, hell-bent on accomplishing their duty to destroy all that which is determined to be an affront to Islam, brutalize an Egyptian, one of their own yet a daily reminder of how Islam had yet to attain supremacy even in its strongholds.

Yes, democracy may have triumphed in Egypt in the so-called "Arab Spring," but that in itself may be the greatest threat to the Christians and other minorities as well as for neighboring Israel. For Christians in Egypt and other Muslim countries affected by this movement, the hopes birthed by the "Arab Spring" are tempered by fears that the reality foreshadows a cold, deadly winter for the minorities. Muslim extremists have kept a low profile, but the majority of Egyptian Muslims support the imposition of sharia law. As a result, Muslim extremists stand poised to assume power "legitimately" through the democratic process, just like the Nazis did in Germany in the early part of the 20th century. The ability of Western countries to object to such a result, and with it the security of over 10 million minority Egyptians, can be seriously compromised if our leaders do not take a strong stand for true democracy and against fascist extremist forces from the start.

Egyptian authorities must recognize the persecution of Christians in the country and provide adequate security to the Christian community. Our Western governments must demand nothing less from the current military authorities or from any future government and they must ensure that the process of establishing a permanent government does not provide a means for Muslim extremists to solidify control of the country.

Whether you are Christian yourself, follow another religion, or are atheist, please stand with your Egyptian sisters and

see the work of Dalia Ziada on the inside story of the Arab Spring and how Egypt can work toward true democracy.

brothers—Christian, Baha'i, and others—the future of Egypt and its minorities is at stake. Egypt desperately needs change—it must move forward into an era of freedom, human rights, and democracy. However, before we make democracy our new idol, we must never forget that democracy brought Hamas to Gaza and Hitler to Germany. Let's do what we can to make sure there is no repeat of these tragedies in Egypt.

As horrific as Ms. Logan's experiences were, they nonetheless give us hope. One woman was all it took—one woman dressed all in black, who had the courage to stand alone against a frenzied mob until other women joined her and formed a wall around Ms. Logan to protect her. They did not need to risk their lives for this stranger and foreigner when they could be killed on the spot themselves by the mob or face repercussions later. But they did. They recognized her humanity and her distress and risked everything to save her. Each one of us can be a "woman in black" for Christians, Baha'is, Ahmadi Muslims, and others in Egypt and around the world. Will we risk our comfort, even our lives, to stand in the gap for our brothers and sisters, whatever their nationality, religion, or beliefs, in order to affirm their humanity and their right to live in accordance with their beliefs and their conscience? Our answer to this question will reveal our own individual humanity.

———◄o►———

While Neha's mother and older sister and brother were busy with chores around the house, Neha wandered outside and found a stick to play with. As she sat by herself, intent at making circles and lines in the dirt, she heard footsteps coming toward her. The toddler looked up to see if Daddy was coming home early from the farm. No, it wasn't Daddy, it wasn't anyone she knew. And when he started running toward her, the look in his eyes made her afraid. He grabbed Neha and ran off before her mommy or anyone heard her cry out.

3

CHINA

"Tell us the names of the other Christians!" the prison guards demanded. At that point we were about 24,000 strong—worshiping our Savior under the cover of darkness, in the shadows so not to endanger each other. Our faith in Jesus as the Son of God brought us strength and courage to endure the daily humiliations and even persecution. That faith is what kept me sane and strong during the seven days of torture and abuse—that faith and God's miraculous kindness in letting me know that I was not alone, and that He would be with me even in the midst of all manner of physical and psychological abuse. When the officer unleashed three vicious attack dogs on me in my tiny cell on day three, I looked up, stunned to find all three dogs seated around me as if they were trying to tell me that God had ordered them not to hurt me. Disgusted, the officer came back with three other dogs but these three took up the exact same positions except that one of them leaned over and licked my face. What a source of strength that small incident was for the days to follow...

I REMEMBER VIVIDLY MY DISAPPOINTMENT in 2001 when the International Olympic Committee (IOC) announced that the 2008 Summer Games would be in China. My sense of disillusionment at the betrayal of the free world and of the Chinese people's hopes for freedom, human rights, and dignity was real. When the world was spellbound watching athletes compete for Olympic fame and glory in Beijing, Chinese Christians were suffering for their beliefs in secret.

One Free World International and I do not believe it was proper to award the Games to China before proof of concrete progress in the government's human rights record. However, because we believed the Chinese people deserved the opportunity to host the Games, we waited to see the government's response before speaking out. China's brutal occupation of Buddhist Tibet and repression of the Falun Gong have received a fair amount of attention over the years. However, Chinese Christians' suffering goes mostly unnoticed in the West. The situation did not improve but worsened in the months before the Games.

Christians in China number about 80 million, or about 6 percent of the 1.3 billion population, and are permitted to worship only in churches controlled by the atheistic, communist government. Any religious activity outside such government-controlled organizations is forbidden, yet an estimated 60 million Christians worship illegally in house churches. While the situation varies across the country, Christians worshiping in house churches and their leaders do so risking harassment, raids, confiscation of religious materials, detention and arrest, physical abuse and torture, and "re-education" in forced labor camps as do adherents of other religions and belief systems who do not choose to toe the communist party line.

INTERNATIONALLY INFAMOUS

China has long been infamous for the treatment of its citizens— born and unborn. Most Westerners know of the one-child-only family policy, which world leaders tend to ignore. Also ignored is the brutality against religion in China, particularly Christians and Falun Gong believers. Persecution of Muslims in China has escalated since 2014

Falun Gong is a controversial Chinese spiritual movement that was founded by Li Hongzhi in 1992. Falun Gong's teachings draw from the Asian religious traditions of Buddhism, Taoism, Confucianism, and Chinese folklore as well as those of Western New Age movements. Adherents exercise ritually to obtain mental and spiritual renewal. The sudden emergence of Falun Gong in the 1990s caused great concern for the Chinese government, which viewed it as a cult and felt threatened by its sudden emergence, broad appeal, and ability to influence and quickly mobilize masses of Chinese citizens outside of the control of the Communist Party. By 1999 there was a reported 70-100 million Falun Gong followers in China.

The 2011 U.S. Commission on International Religious Freedom, a federal body appointed by the president and congressional leaders, states :

> The Chinese government maintains that the Falun Gong movement is a "cult," effectively banning that organization and "justifying" its ongoing brutal crackdown against the movement and its followers. According to Falun Gong practitioners in the United States, in the last four years, over 100,000 practitioners have been sent to labor camps without trial, and over 1,000 have been tortured in mental hospitals, including 430 who have been killed as a result of police brutality. According to the Falun Gong, the Chinese government has continued to pressure foreign businesses in China to discriminate against its followers. Many local officials in foreign countries also stated that they had received warnings from Chinese diplomatic personnel to withdraw their support of Falun Gong and its practitioners.[1]

A book titled *Bloody Harvest* claims that tens of thousands of Falun Gong practitioners have been killed so their internal organs could be sold for transplants.[2]

CHINA'S FALUN GONG CRACKDOWN

Lizhi He was held in a Chinese prison for $3\frac{1}{2}$ years because he confessed to being a Falun Gong believer. He told me that he was repeatedly stripped naked and shocked with an electric baton. He is an example of all the Falun Gong adherents who are kept prisoner and forced to labor in fields and in factories that make products for export to other countries. While suffering from a high fever for months on end, Lizhi was forced to perform heavy labor in the fields—almost to the point of death, and to work on products for export, stitching footballs and making medicines.

"In the face of such horrific brutality, with the world's most powerful authoritarian regime turning the full force of its repressive apparatus against them, Falun Gong practitioners...have responded with one of the largest, most innovative nonviolent movements the world has ever seen. Falun Gong adherents remain among those most severely persecuted in China," Amnesty International wrote about the malfeasance.[3]

One Free World International stands against all religious persecution, and when the Falun Gong Association of Canada organized a parade to bring awareness to the plight of their fellow believers in China, One Free World International marched along beside them the entire route.

Since 2001, it has been reported that Falun Gong members have been killed so that their livers, kidneys, and other vital organs can be sold for very high prices. It is suspected that Falun Gong adherents have been killed "on demand" if their body tissue matches. The organs are sold to either Chinese nationals who are wealthy enough to pay the price or to people from other countries who then fly home with a healthy liver or kidney. According to a report by David Matas and the Honorable David Kilgour, between the period 2000-2005, approximately 41,500 unexplained transplants are estimated to have taken place in China.[4]

SECRETIVE PERSECUTION

According to an article in the *Guardian* by Foreign Affairs Editor Peter Beaumont on July 18, 2009, the daughter of two Falun Gong followers and a former detainee tell of continuing abuse 10 years after China launched its crackdown in 1999. I urge you to read this article because I believe it is representative of many more "detainees" and their families—people about whom the world should not forget.[5]

CHRISTIANS, TOO

Not only are the Falun Gong followers persecuted in China, but Christians as well. In December 2011, one of the largest house congregations held its last outdoor worship service on Christmas Day. It was reported by local Christians that other congregations had been raided by Chinese security forces as part of a Christmas season crackdown and that the Beijing-based Shouwang Church would not continue to worship publicly because authorities had detained dozens of congregants and denied them access to a building the congregation had bought.

Worthy News reported "Shouwang Church had her 37th Sunday outdoor worship service," last week, however, "As Christmas is approaching, each police station puts more force in guarding and watching believers. As far as we know, on Sunday morning, [December 18, 2011] at least 35 believers were taken away [by police] for going to the planned location to join the outdoor service, either at the spot or on their way there." Hours later they were released, but the fear and danger had been felt.

Christmas celebrations were halted in two other provinces where police reportedly raided the main house church December 23 in

Gaoxue village in Dazhu county while believers prepared for a Christmas service. Police allegedly grabbed believers and confiscated the church's musical instruments. Five believers were taken to the police station.

Elsewhere on December 23, members of a house church in Dongyang county, were preparing for their Christmas meeting when they were attacked by police and threatened and told that they must not hold any Christmas celebrations on Christmas Eve.

Chinese officials have consistently denied wrongdoing, saying Christians can worship freely in state-approved Protestant and Catholic denominations. Many of China's more than 80 million Christians prefer to worship outside Communist government control however.[6]

The difference between China, on the one hand, and the United States, Canada, and most European countries, on the other, is similar to night and day when it comes to religious freedom. People in Western, developed nations are naïve or uninformed when realizing the vast freedoms and blessings they enjoy. When it comes to the U.S. Constitution, the framers' first amendment states that:

> Congress shall make no law respecting an establishment of religion, or prohibiting the free exercise thereof; or abridging the freedom of speech, or of the press; or the right of the people peaceably to assemble, and to petition the Government for a redress of grievances.

The founders of the United States knew the importance of freely practicing religion, speaking freely, writing without fear of reprisal, the importance for people to assemble peaceably, and for the people's voices to be heard when wrongs were committed. The very first amendment afforded these freedoms. Is it any wonder that people are legally and illegally immigrating to the United States and other "free" nations?

One such man, Yu Jie, fled China after being abused and tortured—for being a Christian who wrote about issues that the government didn't approve.

In a statement at a press conference in Washington, DC, Yu Jie, former vice president of the Independent Chinese PEN Centre,[7] told about his torture by the Chinese security police after being kidnapped on December 9, 2010, the day before the award ceremony for fellow Chinese writer Liu Xiaobo's Nobel Peace Prize.[8]

On January 11, 2012, Yu and his wife and son boarded a plane to the United States. He plans to publish a biography of Liu Xiaobo and is also writing a book about the Hu Jintao era. Yu was born in 1973 and received a Master's degree from Peking University in 2000. He worked at the National Museum of Modern Chinese Literature until his dismissal and then turned to writing full-time. He is a member of the Beijing Ark Church, a Protestant house church. In May 2006, Yu met with U.S. President George W. Bush at the White House as a dissident and a house church practitioner.[9]

Yu's press statement, "Exposing CPC Tyranny and Running to the Free World: My Statement on Leaving China," translated and released by Human Rights in China at Yu's request[10] is a very interesting and personal look at China's stance against freedoms.

THE PRICE OF HUMAN DIGNITY

The International Olympic Committee failed its own mandate by granting the Games to China despite its well-documented failures on human rights and lack of clear commitment to change. This is not simply a political issue—China's human rights abuses make a mockery of the values highlighted in the Olympic Charter that include "the preservation of human dignity," and "a spirit of friendship, solidarity and fair play." Moreover, the violations spilled over into the Games where the IOC also failed to require China to live up to international standards of human rights and Olympic tradition.

Every Western home today contains products made in China. Yet, the price of human dignity is high compared to the cost of inexpensive products that may have been produced by forced labor. As a result, since the Beijing Olympic Games took place, OFWI has encouraged our friends and partners not to purchase Chinese products and to let China know that the boycott will end when we see proof that China is respecting the religious freedom of its Christians and other minorities—in fact, not just words.

We recognize that the immediate effects of our boycott are akin to those of a pebble thrown in the ocean. But every shopping trip affords the potential of multiple opportunities to share with store clerks why we will not purchase products that are made in China, giving the store an incentive to source its merchandise elsewhere in order to secure our business and educating the clerks about what is happening in China. And perhaps one day even the ripples of a pebble thrown in the ocean will be felt thousands of miles away when China finally takes real steps to respect the human rights of its citizens.

———◄○►———

Holding Neha tightly and roughly in his arms, the man ran down the road and into a field. There he dropped her on the ground and abused her sexually. The little girl cried and bled as he took complete advantage of her innocence and helplessness.

4

AFGHANISTAN

I regained consciousness in a hospital bed and couldn't move. For three months I slowly regained my strength until I was released from the hospital and put under house arrest for another eight long months. Then I was tipped off that I had received a death sentence for my "crimes," so I escaped and hid with a Bedouin family for two months in Sinai. I was afraid for my life and the lives of the kind family who took me in, fed me, and kept me safe. I knew I couldn't stay there indefinitely, so I began developing a plan to flee to Israel, the only safe route of escape.

IN TODAY'S WORLD, THE WORST place for religious freedom is Afghanistan—and the persecution began there long before the start of the current conflict in October 2001 when the United States, the United Kingdom, Australia, and the Afghan United Front (Northern Alliance) launched Operation Enduring Freedom in response to the September 11, 2001, attacks on the United States. The goal of the Operation was to dismantle al Qaeda, a terrorist organization, and end its use of Afghanistan as a base. Removing the Taliban regime from power and creating a viable democratic state was also a goal. Ten years later, the war rages on with few signs of either goal being truly met.

Because of the ongoing, unpredictable violence, when I traveled to Kabul in 2009 to discuss religious freedom issues with Afghan government officials, the members of our team wore bullet proof vests. The city and countryside were pockmarked with bomb remnants and bullet holes; poor and bedraggled little children with big beautiful eyes sat in front of crumbling buildings. At the many security checkpoints, heavily armed soldiers verified our papers and waved us on to the next posted area.

I met with the Deputy Minister of Foreign Affairs for Afghanistan and although he and his staff were open to discuss women's rights and gay rights, there was no discussion allowed regarding Christianity and those who have converted from Islam to become Christians. Government officials continue to publicly condemn conversions and pursue arrests of any and all Muslims who convert to Christianity. Government officials have publicly said that Christians "must be stoned to death" because they are trying to convert Muslims.

How ironic that the Westerners, those "Christian infidels" in the eyes of many Afghans, are the ones who are militarily and financially supporting Afghanistan—assisting the Afghans to become what we hope will be a free and prosperous country. For ten years we have sent our soldiers to help Afghanistan—and thousands of those soldiers have paid an unthinkable personal price while almost 3,000 have made the ultimate sacrifice, dying in their efforts to secure a better future for this hurt and suffering people.

Yet the Deputy Chairman of the Afghanistan Parliament, Abdul Satar Khawasee, had the temerity to say in Parliament, "When the dirty feet of these foreigners reached and stepped in our country, all kinds of religions and national disasters and plagues came to our country."

Some of the comments told to us by typical men on the streets of Kabul included comments like, "The Afghanistan government should take serious measures against these treacherous actions!" He was referring to Muslims converting to Christianity. "They should arrest all those NGOs which are involved in spreading Christianity!" And, "Those who became infidels, they should be punished according to Islamic sharia law!" Sharia law's remedy for Muslim converts to Christianity—execution.

We knocked on politicians' doors every day we were there telling them the seriousness of religious freedom and the need for reform. We did what we could. Unfortunately, the world and politicians are more interested in economic than human rights—especially religious human rights. The faith community worldwide needs to pressure governments, politicians, leaders, and representatives to tie economic aid and trade to improving the treatment of the citizenry of countries such as Afghanistan.

DANGER FOR CONVERTS

At the end of 2010, One Free World International sent out an alert about Said Musa, an Afghan Christian convert who was arrested in the spring of 2010, along with two dozen others, in the course of a public campaign by the Afghan government to find and execute all Afghan converts. As a result of intense international pressure, Said Musa was freed and obtained asylum in a Western country—but his family remains in danger. During his imprisonment, Musa suffered painful physical and emotional abuse. He was pressured to recant his faith—which he refused to do.

During that time the U.S. State Department wrote in its annual International Religious Freedom Report that "respect for religious freedom" decreased in Afghanistan in the last year, "particularly toward Christian groups and individuals." Christians, Hindus, and Sikhs—as well as Muslims whose practices don't satisfy the government or society—suffer "intolerance in the form of harassment, occasional violence, discrimination and inflammatory public statements," the report said. It estimated the Afghan Christian community ranges from 500 to 8,000 people.[1]

For all practical purposes, there are no native Afghan Christians; they are all converts from Islam who worship in secret to avoid being killed for apostasy. The ongoing campaign against converts adds a new, intentional dimension to the persecution of Afghan Christians. This campaign began on May 27, 2010, when a television program claiming to show converts being baptized and praying triggered public demonstrations against converts. In response, pledges were made in the Afghan parliament and supported by President Karzai himself that all Afghan Christians would be found and executed and Christian aid organizations involved in converting Afghans would be punished.

Many other Christians who have been arrested since the broadcast remain in prison, including a man named Shoaib Asadullah whose case is expected to be brought before the court. Asadullah has been attacked and threatened by fellow prisoners and we have continuing grave concerns for his safety. As I write these words, One Free World International is taking active measures to save his life.

FATES OF NON-MUSLIMS AND WOMEN

For more than a year, an Afghan man, a Sikh, was imprisoned after the British government deported him. While in prison in Afghanistan, he says that other inmates and guards taunted, harassed, and beat him for being a Sikh. Sikhs represent a vanishing religious minority in Afghanistan, a deeply conservative Muslim country. The day after *The Washington Post* published a story about the man's plight, Baljit Singh was released. Afghan officials have given him documents that allow him to travel within the country, but have not yet conceded that he is an Afghan citizen. They suspect he is Indian, but have not substantiated that claim. His defense lawyer is trying to find a country willing to admit him as a refugee.[2]

It was reported worldwide about the 15-year-old Afghan child bride who was tortured by her husband's family for not becoming a prostitute. She was "locked in a dark basement bathroom with barely enough food and water to survive," beaten, burned, and had her fingernails pulled out. Afghan health minister Dr. Suraya Dalil visited her in a Kabul hospital and said, "This is one of the worst cases of violence against Afghan women. The perpetrators must be punished so others learn a lesson." Unfortunately, this is an example of increased cases of violence against women in Afghanistan. Fortunately, three of the abusers were sentenced to 10 years in prison for their crimes.[3]

Women continue to suffer in Afghanistan despite billions of dollars of international aid which has poured into the country during the decade-long war. The Afghan Independent Human Rights Commission logged 1,026 cases of violence against women in the second quarter of 2011 compared with 2,700 cases for the whole of 2010. And according to figures in an Oxfam report in October, 87 percent of Afghan women report having experienced physical, sexual or psychological violence or forced marriage. Gul's case comes after a woman known as Gulnaz was pardoned and released earlier in December after spending two years in prison for "moral crimes." She was jailed after she reported to police that her cousin's husband had raped her. Gulnaz gave birth to the rapist's child in prison.

THE BLOODY REALITY

Friends, we must help these people! Our men and women have died to bring peace, freedom, human rights, and dignity to the people of Afghanistan. As of February 10, 2012, there have been a total of 2,885 coalition forces killed—including 1,893 U.S. soldiers, 158 Canadian soldiers, and 397 U.K. soldiers—who have shed their blood on foreign soil in these past ten years, and more than 15,000 U.S. soldiers have been wounded and maimed for life. Yet the government of Afghanistan—not the Taliban, not al Qaeda, but the Karzai government—tramples on our soldiers' blood and tells its citizens at gunpoint what they may and may not believe!

Those who continue to be held by Afghan authorities for converting to Christianity must be released immediately and their safety ensured. The Afghan government must immediately cancel its anti-Christian policies, repudiate its statements about converts, and set about to ensure respect for the religious freedom of all of its citizens. It is not acceptable that Christians are exiled from their land or face the alternative of death, like Said Musa and Shoaib Asadullah, simply because of what they choose to believe.

When I returned from Afghanistan, I spoke before the Canadian members of parliament and shared with them compelling evidence of human rights abuses there. On November 30, 2010, I testified before the Subcommittee on International Human Rights of the Canadian Parliament's Standing Committee on Foreign Affairs and International Development.[4] My testimony centered on three issues that dominated my visit to Afghanistan. First I discussed the impact on women's rights of the recent passing of a discriminatory and even abusive personal status law for shi'a Muslims. Then I spoke about the sexual slavery and abuse of young Afghan boys by powerful men—a practice called bacha bazi. Finally, I highlighted a focused and deliberate campaign that was undertaken by the Afghan government to find and execute converts to Christianity.

Joining our voices with millions of others around the world, we helped secure Said Musa's release. We must ensure that our governments continue to keep up the pressure on Afghanistan. Afghan Muslims must be able to choose their own beliefs, whether that means holding on to their Muslim beliefs or converting to

Christianity or any other religion of their choice, and they must be free to live and exercise their chosen beliefs in safety in their homeland.

"When I came home from working at the farm that day, I noticed that Neha was gone, so I went to look for my little girl. As I searched frantically in the fields around our home, I saw a young man in the field. I recognized him—it was my employer's son—and he was raping my Neha! When he saw me, he turned and ran away. I ran to Neha who was unconscious. I wanted to run after and catch the man, but when I saw my daughter unconscious and bleeding, I was not able to even go any farther. I took her in my arms and, cradling her bruised and broken body, I wept bitterly as I carried her home."

5

ISRAEL

Making my way past the tourists and hotel security staff at the Hilton in Taba (a resort town on the Red Sea near the Egypt/Israel border), I saw my ticket to freedom—a jet ski. I paid the fellow at the rental counter a few Egyptian pounds for the rental and then, careful not to draw attention to myself, I climbed aboard, turned the key, and when the engine roared to life, I steered it across the water and landed a short distance away in Israel, in front of the Princess Hotel in the city of Eilat. There were no cheers or welcoming parade...rather, I surrendered to the nearest Israeli officer who was clearly on alert, unable to determine if I was a terrorist. And here I am, in prison once again, although this cell bears no comparison with the torture section of Abu Zaabel. Because of the peace treaty with Egypt, Israel cannot take me in. Legally, I cannot stay in Israel; yet if they send me back, I will be executed.

THE BIRTHPLACE OF THE JEWISH people is the Land of Israel (Eretz Yisrael), and it is where a significant part of the nation's long history was enacted, of which the first thousand years are recorded in the Bible. In that Land is where the Jewish people's cultural, religious, and national identity was formed; and there, its physical presence has been maintained through the centuries, even after the majority was forced into exile. During the many years of dispersion, the Jewish people never severed nor forgot its bond with the Land. With the establishment of the State of Israel in 1948, Jewish independence, lost 2,000 years earlier, was renewed.[1]

But living in Israel has never been easy; neighboring countries and terrorist organizations daily threaten Israel's safety and security. For example, Iran's leader, Mahmud Ahmadinejad, publicly denies the Holocaust—when 6 million Jews were murdered by Nazis who viewed them as a biological threat to the purity of the German race—and Iran continues to be the only country that has openly called for the annihilation of the State of Israel. President Ahmadinejad actively endorses chaos, so as to hasten the re-emergence of Islam's Hidden Imam—or the Twelfth Imam, the Shiites' great spiritual savior—and spread true Islamic rule worldwide. He believes that the Hidden Imam will return only following an apocalyptic war against Israel and the West.[2]

HAMAS ATTACKS

In a CBN News interview in January 2010, I reported that Christians were being attacked on an almost daily basis in Gaza. An example of this became worldwide news in February 2011 when a prominent Christian surgeon in the Gaza Strip had a bomb thrown at his car. No one was hurt in the incident, but it served as a warning that was followed by text messages telling Dr. Maher Ayyad to stop his evangelical work or face the consequences. Christians in Gaza have faced increased persecution since Hamas wrested control of the area in June 2007 during a violent coup to enforce the results of an election it had won. Since taking control, Hamas has been instituting sharia law that effectively forbids any non-Muslims from talking about their faith.

Christians living in Gaza face persecution—their homes and churches are attacked almost everyday. Christian schools have also been attacked, vehicles torched, equipment stolen, and school personnel threatened. In October 2007, Islamists murdered Rami Ayad, an Arab Christian who worked at the Palestinian Bible Society.

There are about 3,500 Christians in Gaza—among 1.4 million Muslims. After the takeover, Hamas dug up Christian graves and burned the bodies because they felt the remains defiled the land. Shortly after Hamas seized control we received reports of two kinds of violations: 1) Hamas was torturing the members of Fatah in Gaza and 2) Hamas was going to the graveyards of the Christians, digging up the dead bodies of Christians, throwing them, burning them, and saying, "You cannot bury your dead bodies here because it's our land, it's a holy land. By burying your Christian families here you are desecrating the land." One Free World International received such reports about five different grave sites in Gaza.

We also received reports about Christian families being forced to cooperate with Hamas or their children or their wives would be raped or persecuted. So they were forced to cooperate.

The Palestinian Authority itself is just as determined to get rid of the Christians, if not as open about its goals. The Palestinian Authority wants support from the West, so the leaders try to portray themselves as a "democratic country." But Bethlehem, the city of Jesus' birth, where there has been a steady exodus of the Christian community for decades, is a good example of this façade. Bethlehem has become a "tourist zone" for the Palestinian Authority. Basically they don't want the Christians there, but they want the Christian tourists to come and spend their money.

I believe that the future of Christians in the Muslim world is, in large part, dependent on Western Christians doing their part to confront evil. From the horror of the Holocaust to the massacres of Darfur, people have not done enough to stop the terror.

Christians should pray every day for the persecuted Church, for Christian soon-to-be martyrs, for people of faith in communist, Muslim, and closed countries. I encourage you to take action by going to your federal government representatives or parliamentarians to raise the issue. In many cases, Western countries are giving aid to countries that persecute Christian minorities. Westerners should demand that their governments tie international aid to improvements in human rights.

WHILE SLEEPING

The world was shocked when the report was aired about terrorists who infiltrated the West Bank settlement of Itamar and stabbed to death five members of the Fogel family—Udi (36) and Ruth (35), and their children Yoav, 11; Elad, 4; and 3-month-old Hadas. The killings occurred on March 11, 2011, when one or two attackers jumped the fence that surrounds Itamar and broke into the Fogel home. The murderers went from room to room, first stabbing the parents and their 3-month-old baby girl. They proceeded to the next room where they killed the two sleeping boys. Two other boys were sleeping in another room and were not attacked. The family's oldest child, 12-year-old Tamar, was out of the house at the time and alerted neighbors when no one opened the door for her.

Prime Minister Benjamin Netanyahu said about the murders,

> "I expect a similar condemnation, and I demand a similar condemnation, from the Palestinian Authority. I am disappointed by the weak and mumbled statements. This is not how one condemns terrorism. This is not how one fights terrorism. See how Israeli prime ministers, myself among them, have reacted in similar situations, but there has never been anything like this, in which terrorists entered a home and cut children's throats.

"This requires sharp and unequivocal condemnation. This requires something else. This requires a halt to the incitement. I demand that the Palestinian Authority stop the incitement that is conducted on a daily basis in their schools, mosques and the media under their control. The time has come to stop this double-talk in which the Palestinian Authority outwardly talks peace, and allows—and sometimes leads—incitement at home. The time has come to stop the incitement and begin educating their people for peace."[3]

The terrorism is not only about land, it is about anti-Semitism, about Muslims unwilling to exist side by side with Jews.

SO THE WORLD WILL KNOW AND REMEMBER

When the Canadian Parliamentary Coalition to Combat Anti-Semitism instituted an inquiry into anti-Semitism in Canada in 2009, they invited me to testify about how anti-Semitism in Canada relates to anti-Semitism elsewhere in the world and to the broader question of religious persecution globally. The written report I submitted is reproduced in Appendix D, but my oral statement is worth reproducing in full here. It will give you important insight into the connections between anti-Semitism and religious persecution in the broader sense and help you understand why I, as an Egyptian Christian convert, take every opportunity to stand up for the Jewish people and for the right of the state of Israel to defend itself and its people against those who would seek to destroy them. As I told the inquiry,

Anti-Semitism is a despicable, evil attitude that leads to untold suffering. Throughout the ages it has demonized the Jewish people to justify discrimination, abuse, and even murder. It is a road that ends seeking the destruction of the Jewish people, as in the Nazi Holocaust.

From the exile of the Jewish people by the Romans after the destruction of the temple in Jerusalem to the horror of the Nazi gas chambers, Jews have been persecuted, harassed, and even killed simply because they are Jewish.

While there are no Nazi death camps today, anti-Semitism is rising not just here in Canada but also around the world. Just in 2005, in Paris, a Jewish young man, 23 years old, was kidnapped, was tortured for 24 days, and was killed in the end. Twenty-three people were arrested; 23 people were involved directly and indirectly in his case.

Close to home, here in Canada, synagogues and schools have been vandalized and fire-bombed, from Montreal and Quebec City to Kelowna, British Columbia, while university students hide their Jewish identity to avoid harassment and intimidation on campuses such as York University and Concordia in Montreal.

In my opinion, there are two reasons for the problem of rising anti-Semitism here in Canada today. Number one, the new wave of anti-Semitism is hiding under or wearing the mask of anti-Zionists. Today it's more politically correct, if I may say so, to attack Israel. Instead of attacking the Jewish people and instead of anti-Semitism, today it's much easier to attack the state of Israel or the Israelis themselves.

So the new wave of anti-Semitism today in our world is wearing the anti-Zionist mask. This does not mean that we don't have the right to criticize the state of Israel or their policy. The state of Israel, like any other state, deserves to be criticized for their policy, but based on fact and truth, not just propaganda. Today the thin line that I'm concerned about with the rising of the anti-Zionists is that we're taking from the Jewish people their right to defend themselves and the acknowledged existence of the state of Israel.

What I'm saying here is that this new wave of anti-Semitism, wearing the mask of the anti-Zionist, is taking away from the Israeli people or from the Jewish people their ability to understand that they have the right to exist or to defend themselves, but not to criticize Israel. We can criticize Israel as a country and their policy. I am one of the people who criticizes Israel with regard, for example, to their policy concerning the Christians and Palestinians, but this does not mean taking away the right to exist or to defend themselves. Just a few weeks ago in Canada, The United Church of Canada rejected a resolution mandating a boycott of Israel, but passed another one encouraging individual groups and churches to examine the issue and take the proper measures. It's as though they are trying to have their cake and eat it too.

This is the first problem we are facing, which is the rise of anti- Zionism, and hiding behind it is anti-Semitism.

The second problem we are facing is political correctness.

Political correctness is right now here in Canada, such as in the media, for example, or with the politicians, or even academics. In the old days the job of the media was to report the truth and the facts on the ground. The politicians would stand for the truth, for the facts. But today in the media, or in politics or academia, they need to balance. They need to be politically correct.

Now when you watch the news they need to balance between the conflicts so they don't upset either group. But this is not really the job of the media. The media should not be politically correct. The media is supposed to publish the facts and the truth. It is the same for the politicians. Some politicians make their decisions based on which group in their riding, for example, will give them more votes. This is not supposed to be the case. They are supposed to support the facts and the truths on the ground.

Those are the two main problems that I believe are the reason for the rise in anti-Semitism.

Ladies and gentlemen, without taking more of your time, I am not here today just to fight anti-Semitism. I am here fighting anti- Semitism, and I am not a Jewish man; I am an Egyptian man. But I have learned through my experiences in the Middle East that when there is anti-Semitism anywhere, there is also persecution of other minorities.

For example, Egypt is a country that had a peace agreement at Camp David with Israel for over 25 years. Today their schools and their media are all anti-Semitic. It is all propaganda.

When I was nine years old and in school—and I remember this like yesterday—my history teacher stood in front of me and he was teaching us that we must hate the Jewish people. As a nine-year-old in Egypt I stood in front of him and I asked him, why do we need to hate them if we already have a peace agreement with them? Why are we talking about war? As my punishment, he beat my hands with a stick, on this hand five times and on this hand five times.

Fair enough. Eleven years later, when I became a Christian in Egypt I was persecuted; I was tortured for my beliefs.

In Iran, a country where they threaten every day to wipe Israel off the map, they persecute Christians, and the Bahá'ís. In Pakistan, a country that doesn't even acknowledge the state of Israel's existence, they have persecution of Ahmadis, of Christians. They have slave camps for the minorities.

The persecution that is happening, or the anti-Semitism that is happening, today to the Jewish people is not just affecting the Jewish people. If we let this happen here in Canada, and if we let anti-Semitism rise in Canada, we will be next. The Bahá'ís will be next, the Ahmadis will be next, the Christians will be next.

So we need to stand up today for the Jewish people and to fight anti-Semitism. We need to educate our public. We need to lose political correctness. We need to mention the facts and not to focus on propaganda, not just for the sake of the Jewish people but for the sake of every minority.

We need to remember that in 1937, the ship, St. Louis, came to the shores of this country. It was filled with 900 Jews. Our Prime Minister at the time, Mackenzie King, used to ask his dog for foreign affairs advice and talk to his mother's ghost. That's a true story; it's a fact. He sent them back, and most of them were killed by the Nazis. We need to ensure that this will never again happen in our history. Canada is the temple of human rights and is the conscience of this world. We need to be sure that this will never happen again.[4]

Indeed, we must be sure that this will never happen again. We must be sure that it will not happen to the Jews, or to the Christians, or to the Baha'is, or the Ahmadis, or the Falun Gong, or the Sabean-Mandaeans, or anyone else. This is our challenge today.

———————◄○►———————

When the doctors saw Neha's little battered and bleeding body, her parents could see the look in their eyes—their little girl was seriously hurt and suffering. Emergency care was only able to treat Neha's immediate medical needs. She would need much more care and lengthy, complicated surgeries. But news of the attack spread quickly through the countryside. The employer's family and local Muslim extremists began to use their influence, and Neha was turned away from hospital after hospital. Finally, under pressure from OFWI and Neha's other international supporters, additional medical attention was secured. Neha—less than three years old—was in the hospital for months and endured five surgeries to repair the damage done to internal organs. A 12-inch scar crosses her abdomen, and she will never be able to urinate normally. The horror of the vicious attack haunts her memory, she cries out at night...

6

IRAN AND IRAQ

I was in an Israeli prison for one year, three months, fifteen days, twelve hours, and 24 minutes. Unlike the prison in Egypt, this place and the guards were not torturous—but when in prison, you count every minute of lost freedom. After calling and writing letters and reaching out to anyone, any organization who would listen, with the help of Amnesty International, the International Christian Embassy Jerusalem, and the United Nations, I was eventually accepted as a political refugee by the UN High Commissioner for Refugees and released to freedom in Israel. I lived in Jerusalem for the next year and a half as I sought a more secure place to make my new life. Finally, one day I received the news I had been waiting for—I had been granted political asylum in Canada.

IRAN

IN 2005, THE NEW PRESIDENT of Iran, Mahmoud Ahmadinejad said, "Anybody who recognizes Israel will burn in the fire of the Islamic nation's fury, [while] any [Islamic leader] who recognizes the Zionist regime means he is acknowledging the surrender and defeat of the Islamic world." Ahmadinejad was addressing a conference titled The World Without Zionism. "There is no doubt that the new wave [of attacks] in Palestine will wipe off this stigma [Israel] from the face of the Islamic world." Recalling the late Ayatollah Rùhollah Khomeini, leader of Iran's Islamic revolution, Ahmadinejad said, "As the imam said, Israel must be wiped off the map."[1]

Six years later, the president of Iran is no less adamant about spreading Islam worldwide. In an address to the United Nations in September 2011, he denied the Holocaust, thinks that the United States was complicit in the September 11, 2001, attacks, and believes that the Twelfth Imam's return is imminent.[2]

COURAGE AND FAITH

The Iranian population is 98 percent Muslim, with the remaining 2 percent a mixture of other religions, including Christianity and the Baha'i faith which was born in this region. Despite the roots of the Baha'i faith in Iran, its adherents face routine repressive tactics from the authorities, from policies that effectively exclude them from any form of participation in public life and make even the most basic transactions grounds for arbitrary detention. Baha'is face similar tactics in other countries like Egypt and Iraq, where they exist in tiny minorities and their faith is not recognized by the governments, leading to enormous challenges in the most basic transactions, from obtaining an education or owning property, to marriage and divorce or burying their dead, simply because of their inability to obtain official recognition of their religious status on identity documents.

In March 2009, One Free World International sent out an alert about two courageous Iranian women, Maryam and Marzieh, who were held for almost nine months in prison and suffered abuse because of their Christian faith. These two young converts from Islam were pressured, in court by a prosecutor, to renounce their Christian faith—they refused steadfastly and boldly testified about their relationship with God. In the course of the hearing, the women reportedly indicated that they had become Christians as a result of being convicted by the Holy Spirit. In response, the prosecutor stated, "It is impossible for God to speak with humans," to which Marzieh responded, "Are you questioning whether God is Almighty?" When the prosecutor replied, "You are not worthy for God to speak to you," Marzieh responded, "It is God, and not you, who determines if I am worthy."

After the hearing, Maryam and Marzieh were sent back to Evin prison, an Iranian prison notorious for its abuses and the same prison where Canadian citizen and photojournalist Zahra Kazemi was beaten to death during interrogation in 2003. The two women were told they would be freed when they were ready to comply with the court's demands to renounce their faith.

The women suffered numerous health problems without adequate medical treatment and lost a lot of weight while in prison. They were eventually acquitted of the charges of "anti-state activities" and "taking part in illegal gatherings" and apostasy. If Maryam and Marzieh had been found guilty, they could have faced lengthy imprisonment and further hearings and, ultimately, abusive punishments or death. They were freed thanks in part to our faithful prayer partners and letters sent on their behalf joining voices with thousands of others around the world in support of Maryam and Marzieh. Every voice is important and we were delighted to be able to share in their victory when we received news that they had arrived in a safe third country.

Maryam and Marzieh are just two of many Christians in Iran who have been unjustly imprisoned for their faith. Other minorities, such as the Baha'is, regularly face varying degrees of persecution. In the midst of growing repression, the entire Christian community and other minority communities in Iran need our continued prayers and support. While the government decided not to pass a threatened apostasy law, torture and extrajudicial killings are still common in Iran.

HOUSE CHURCH MOVEMENT CRACKDOWNS

Unfortunately, the Iranian government has orchestrated a deliberate and widespread crackdown on Christians and particularly a growing house church movement in the country. Accurate numbers are difficult to state, but in a wave of arrests at Christmas in 2010 and in early January 2011, approximately 100 people were arrested. Some of these people were released on bail while an unknown number remain in prison where they have faced isolation, brutal interrogation tactics, threats, and other physical and emotional abuse in addition to generally harsh conditions common in Iran's notorious prisons. Even those released on bail are not out of danger as their cases continue through the system and their names remain on file with authorities.

In another wave of arrests in mid-February 2011, some 45 Christians were held overnight to harass and intimidate them. Many were forced to sign papers stating they will not attend church and they may yet face further actions by the authorities. In the meantime, a pastor named Youcef Nadarkhani has been imprisoned since 2009 for apostasy. After three years, he is still awaiting an appeal of a death sentence. After worldwide outrage about his captivity, including letters from supporters of One Free World International to Iranian authorities, in March 2012 an Iranian envoy denied an execution order had been issued for Pastor Nadarkhani. He revealed a list of charges against the evangelical Christian according to which he was guilty of "offending Islam."

According to an article in *The Christian Post,* the Iranian envoy's denial "was prompted by a human rights investigator who openly condemned Iran's imprisonment of Nadarkhani in a 36-page report, presented to several U.N. representatives at the Human Rights Council in Geneva, Switzerland."[3] A representative of Iran's High Council for Human Rights claimed that Pastor Nadarkhani was preaching Christianity to youth that he invited into his home without their parents' permission. He also claims that the pastor converted his home's basement to a church without the government's permission. Although the United States, Germany, Mexico, France, Great Britain, and other countries have openly demanded Pastor Nadarkhani's release,[4] as I write these words, he remains imprisoned and subject to the death sentence because of his faith.

HOUSE CHURCH ARRESTS

In February 2012, Iranian security authorities invaded a house church and arrested Christian converts gathered there to worship.[5] Security officials had previously asked one of the men taken to renounce his faith and collaborate with the intelligence office. Noteworthy is a previous report regarding the arrest of a number of Christians in the Assembly of God church of Ahwaz including the pastor of the church and two other church members. The pressures and security measures implemented by the Islamic Republic against churches in Iran have resulted in the closure of churches. Churches allowed to remain open, are obliged by order of the Intelligence Ministry to prevent Farsi speakers from entering their churches. "In spite of all these circumstances, when people from other religious backgrounds embrace Christianity, they feel the need to gather in small groups in their homes and dedicate their own personal houses for worship services. The Islamic Republic of Iran considers such groups security and spying tools for the west."[6]

Michael Carl, veteran pastor, journalist, and political consultant, wrote an article in February 2012 stating that "persecution of Christians is only growing more bold and brazen, as Iranian authorities once again raided a house church—this time in Shiraz—and arrested between 6 to 10 members of the congregation. The detainees are being held in an undisclosed location." The article quotes *Jihad Watch* publisher Robert Spencer who says that the Iranians don't know that they're doing the very thing that will produce more Christians. "They don't know that Christianity grows amid persecution," Spencer said. "Islam has expanded through violence and intimidation, so it isn't at all surprising that they'd resort to it again."

Also quoted is Clare Lopez, a senior fellow with the Center for Security Policy, who agrees:

> "The issue has little to do with perceptions of how Christianity might respond," Lopez said, "but rather with the obligation under Islamic doctrine to put and keep dhimmis in their 'place' within Muslim society. The forces of Shariah Islam are in the ascendant all over the Middle East these days," Lopez continued, "and with the new-found sense of empowerment combined with what is perceived as Western complicity and weakness in the face of that situation, it is to be expected that all religious minorities, but especially Christians and Jews, increasingly will feel the brutality of Islamic supremecism [sic]." Lopez says Americans need to remember that Islam doesn't focus on "Western" values and political ideas. "Remember, pluralism and tolerance are totally Western ideas, completely foreign to Islam and certainly the Middle East," Lopez said. "Recall that Persian history, aside from the brief interlude of the Pahlavi dynasty in the 20th Century, was one of dynasty, jihad and vicious anti-Semitism.

> "Islam is supremacist, and whenever it feels the ability to dominate and suppress non-Muslims, that is what will occur," Lopez said, "which is completely in accord with the Pact of Umar and Islamic law on treatment of 'People of the Book.' This is from Sura 9.29, the Sura of the Sword. In reality, what we are seeing now is the 'default position' of Islam," Lopez added.

This is not true. My Jewish ancestors lived in the Ottoman Empire in Lebanon, Syria, and Turkey and that was a tolerant and pluralistic society (in most times and places). It all broke down in the lead-up to World War I.

Christianity has also been turned toward violence and oppression or toward peace and cooperation, depending on the time and place.

"Iranian authorities know that Western Church authorities—whether Catholic, Protestant, or others—have not risen to the defense of Egyptian Copts or Iraqi Christians, whose situation has been far worse than what Iranian Christians have faced recently," Lopez said.

Lopez also notes that Iran may feel a slight degree of diplomatic pressure.

"The Iranian regime at one and the same time feels under assault itself (sanctions, nuclear program pressure, Sunni regional enmity and dominance) and still feels confident it can get away with what it's doing to these Christians," Lopez said. "I think we will see this regime lashing out in various and expanding ways as the current Sunni-Shi'ite power rivalry plays out across the Middle East chessboard."

Lopez notes that feeling of pressure, however, will easily disappear if the nuclear program continues to develop on schedule.

"If it is allowed to demonstrate a deliverable nuclear capability, its behavior will become completely impervious to outside influence," Lopez said. "But no one should expect Islamic authorities, who are bursting with confidence in the wake of their takeover of North Africa and with sights now set on Syria, Jordan, Yemen and more, to be responsive to anything but massive publicity combined with credible, serious pressure imposed by the international community.

"Why should they?" she asked. "They think they are on an inexorable, inevitable rise, and they see the West, especially the U.S., actually aiding and supporting their rise to power on the one hand and on the other, falling all over themselves to appease them.

"They see Western-allied Middle Eastern regimes crumbling before them with no meaningful counter response to keep them in check. Even more so in Iran, which expects to be a bona fide nuclear power in the very near future," Lopez said.

Warner also points to another inconsistency between the suffering church worldwide and the North American church: a desire for "religious dialogue."

"This week in a city near you, religious leaders and academics will be at dialog about the Abrahamic faiths," Warner said.

Lopez says that she's not optimistic about the Western churches raising a voice in protest.

"I wish I could say that the Western world once again would rise to the defense of Middle Eastern Christians and other oppressed minorities (don't forget the Iranian Baha'is, who've been brutally suppressed since at least 1979). And any publicity you can give the plight of these Iranian Christians will surely help," Lopez said.[7]

IRAQ

One Free World International routinely and strategically shines the light of Jesus on the darkness pervading the world that is trying to keep His truth and love from His people. One such effort to bring awareness to the plight of the Iraqi Christians is the opinion piece I wrote that was published in *The Ottawa Citizen* newspaper in April 2008, "Canada can do more to help Iraqi Christians":

We would like to thank Jennifer Green and the Citizen for sharing a story that has been largely ignored by Western media. The [Canadian] government's decision to double its refugee allocation from Iraq to 1,800 to 2,000 per year is important, but far from adequate.

The policy that is stated by Tim Vail, spokesman for Citizenship and Immigration Canada, of not singling out "any religious group for special treatment" and relying on the United Nations High Commissioner for Refugees [UNHCR] to recommend who needs our help is hypocritical. *of course, the UN is swayed by the influence of 50+ Muslim countries and their allies.*

It abdicates Canada's responsibility for our own refugee policy and fails to address the unique problems faced by Christians and other minorities, such as Baha'is and Ismailis, especially those who cannot get to UNHCR processing centres in Jordan and Syria.

Obviously, the problem of Iraqi refugees cannot be solved by Canada alone, although concerned Canadians, such as Toronto immigration lawyer Chantal Desloges, are working hard to do their part. However, as a member of the international community, alone and in cooperation with other countries, Canada must take steps to ensure that certain minorities do not bear an unequal share of the cost of this war.

However, this is not just an immigration matter. Canada, through the Department of Foreign Affairs, must hold the Iraqi government accountable for securing the rights of minorities so they do not have to flee.

With $300,000,000 in aid announced since this conflict began and almost $1.8 billion in total trade, Canada must exercise its influence in Baghdad. Our parliamentarians and cabinet ministers must take the lead of Jason Kenney, secretary of state for multiculturalism and Canadian identity, who has taken an active interest in this matter but who cannot resolve it alone.

We must not lose sight of the forgotten victims of the Iraq war nor abandon Canada's ability and duty to help.

Although written for a Canadian audience, these sentiments have been also shared with governments worldwide to keep the light shining on the issues—the life and death issues that face Christians and religious minorities. Jason Kenney has since been appointed Minister for Citizenship and Immigration ensuring a strong voice on religious freedom issues in the Canadian cabinet, but the original point of my opinion piece remains—religious freedom as one of the most fundamental human rights must be recognized and adopted by our politicians in Canada, the United States, and elsewhere in the free world as a fundamental principle informing all our actions both at home and abroad, not just a laudable theoretical statement with no practical effect.

FACE TO FACE IN IRAQ

In September 2011, I led a One Free World International delegation to Iraq to discuss the threats facing Iraqi minorities with high-level government officials including the Vice-President, the Deputy Prime Minister, the President of Parliament (equivalent to the Speaker of the House in Canada or the United States), the Minister of Human Rights, the Minister of the Environment, senior Foreign Affairs officials, and others. Accompanying me as observers were a Canadian member of parliament and a senator, making ours the highest-level Canadian visit to Iraq since the war.

Together with a camera man who was part of our team, I visited Our Lady of Salvation Church in central Baghdad and spoke with and encouraged victims shaken by recent attacks on their communities. Our Lady of Salvation Church itself was the target of a violent hostage-taking in which more than 50 people were killed. The attack was claimed by al-Qaeda's local affiliate, the Islamic State of Iraq. Almost a year after the attack, the church was still an empty shell. Debris was pushed aside but rebuilding had scarcely begun. I spoke with some of the victims and were directed to the vestry where some of the victims had taken refuge. The room was mostly bare, but on the wall was a haunting reminder of the horrors that had taken place here—the bloody handprint of a young woman named Ragda who had died in the attack. She was pregnant.

I spoke to the authorities about this incident, and they continued to cast blame on "foreign elements," denying any responsibility for the events. Yet no one could explain to us why the security detail guarding the church had been removed only hours before the attack or why the security officials who entered the church after the attack stole gold and jewelry and other valuables from the victims. The visit filled me with mixed emotions. The feelings of anger and despair mixed with guilt for not doing enough to prevent these kinds of incidents was overwhelming. At the same time, the desperate need to continue the fight was painfully obvious.

Since 2003, hundreds of thousands of Christians have been driven out of Iraq. Iraq's Christian minority, mainly living in Baghdad, Kirkuk, and Nineveh province, have been targeted in the past. In 2011, there was a violent attack against a church in Kirkuk, and two others were targeted. Twenty-three people were wounded when a car bomb positioned outside a Christian church exploded. Security forces disabled explosives found in other vehicles located outside two additional parishes in northern Iraq. "The terrorists want to make us flee Iraq, but they will fail," said the Rev. Haithem Akram, the priest of one of the targeted churches. "We are staying in our country. The Iraqi Christians are easy targets because they do not have militias to protect them. The terrorists want to terrorize us, but they will fail."[8]

It is estimated that 400,000 to 600,000 Christians remain in Iraq, down from a prewar level of approximately 800,000 or as high as 1.4 million by some estimates, leaving the population reduced to about half that of only 10 years ago. Iraqi Christian churches and communities have been targeted specifically by bombs, kidnappings, and threats, including threats to either convert to Islam, leave, or be killed. Authorities make a show of responding when an attack is too scandalous to ignore, but Iraqi minorities point to indications that the authorities themselves are often complicit in these attacks.

While the impact of the past several years on the Iraqi Christian community is staggering, it pales in comparison with the impact on Sabean-Mandaeans. This close-knit and insular community, whose ancient beliefs include, among other things, the veneration of John the Baptist, exists traditionally in areas of Iraq and Iran and some surrounding areas. Of the estimated worldwide population of about 60,000-70,000, approximately 50,000 lived in pre-2003 Iraq. Today, only an estimated 5,000 remain. They have been forced, through the broader violence and attacks like those facing the Christian community, to seek refuge in various countries outside Iraq. Faced with possible dispersion around the globe, Sabean-Mandaeans face the disintegration of their community, the destruction of their way of life, and the looming extinction of their ancient beliefs.

Yezidis are another ancient community unique to this area of the world. Their 4,000 year-old beliefs involve the worship of certain angels said to have been charged by God after creation with the on-going management of the earth. Despite their strong and ancient roots in the region, the 700,000 or so Iraqi Yezidi community has diminished to an estimated population of 500,000 since 2003.

We may not agree with the beliefs of some communities, but we are not concerned about their beliefs—these are not at issue

Iraq was once even more diverse than its pre-2003 status.
Assyrians were ethnically cleansed during WWI.
Baghdad's population was once 1/3 Jewish, but they were driven out through random arrests, massacres, torture, theft of religious artifacts, etc.

here. On the other hand, we are very concerned about the right of Sabean-Mandaeans, Yezidis, Baha'is, and others in Iraq and everywhere else to hold their peaceful beliefs, whatever they are, and not to change or abandon them unless they choose to, freely and with full opportunity to investigate the options for themselves. If we are not willing to stand with them in their trials today, how can we expect them or anyone else to stand with us tomorrow?

ATTRA

Attra is a young Iraqi Christian refugee who was kidnapped, tortured, and left for dead. Together with his family he is now safe in Canada where we have had the privilege of assisting them in adjusting to their new lives. We sat by Attra's hospital bed one day as this 24-year-old paralyzed man with a cross proudly tattooed on his right arm told us how he had worked for the coalition forces in Iraq. Because of that and his faith in Christ, he was stolen away and beaten unmercifully and "burned with electricity." He showed us the multiple, deep ugly scars on his legs, arms, back, and abdomen from the torture. The kidnappers gave him three options: convert to Islam, kill an American soldier, or pay $250,000. He told us that his captors taunted him over and over saying, "Do you think Jesus will help you? Only your money can help you. If you pay, you go free. If you don't, you are dead!"

Attra told us, "From one second to the next you don't know if you are alive or dead. You don't know if you will ever see people from before, you don't know if you will see your parents, your mom, your dad. You don't know from second to second." He shook his head, "You hear this happening all the time, but to be in the middle of it…when it happens to you personally—it's completely different. Maybe when I am speaking you will only understand half of the idea, but I feel the full impact of it."

Coalition forces were hard-pressed to help or protect the people because any sign of collusion between them and the soldiers would bring harsh consequences or even death for Iraqi Christians. If they helped, the people may be seen as spies or cooperating with the coalition forces.

"NEW IRAQ"

In Washington on December 12, 2011, President Barack Obama and Iraqi Prime Minister Nouri al-Maliki hailed a "new Iraq." But they failed to acknowledge persecution of religious minorities in the country that the United States and other coalition forces helped to liberate. After his meeting with Prime Minister al-Maliki, President Obama told reporters, "People throughout the region will see a new Iraq that's determining its own destiny—a country in which people from different religious sects and ethnicities can resolve their differences peacefully through the democratic process."[9]

But the U.S. Commission on International Religious Freedom (USCIRF), a federal body appointed by the president and congressional leaders, urged the president to take up the issue of religious freedom with the Iraqi prime minister.[10] "Since 2008, and most recently in May 2011, USCIRF has recommended that Iraq should be designated as a 'country of particular concern' under the International Religious Freedom Act for systematic, ongoing, egregious violations of religious freedom," the USCIRF wrote in a letter to President Obama and delivered to him prior to his meeting with al-Maliki.

The letter continues, "Despite an overall decrease in violence in the country, members of Iraq's smallest religious minorities, including Christians, Sabean Mandaeans, and Yazidis continue to suffer from targeted violence, threats, and intimidation, against which the government does not provide effective protection."

Other portions of the USCIRF letter are most telling, as are the U.S. State Department report findings:

For Iraq to become a secure and stable democracy, it must guarantee and enforce the human rights of all Iraqis, both in law and in practice, USCIRF urges you [President Obama] to raise with Prime Minister al-Maliki the urgent need for his government to protect Iraq's most vulnerable religious minority communities, who face the threat of religious cleansing, and ensure them justice. Specifically, the Iraqi government should work with the smallest minorities' political and civic representatives to develop more effective security measures; undertake prompt, transparent, and effective investigations of all human rights violations and bring perpetrators to justice; and address the ongoing problems of discrimination, marginalization and neglect of religious minorities.[11]

In the U.S. State Department's International Religious Freedom report on Iraq, covering July 1-December 31, 2010, Muslim Iraqis who convert to another religion face death. The report reads: "In practice, government institutions do not acknowledge conversion from Islam for official purposes, and persons who leave Islam often face severe social persecution, including death, often by assailants known to the victims."[12]

Also according to the U.S. State Department report:

Iraq's criminal code 201 stipulates that any person promoting Zionist principles, or who associates himself with Zionist organizations or assists them by giving material or moral support, or works in any way toward the realization of Zionist objectives, is subject to punishment by death.

The country has an area of 168,754 square miles and a population of 28.9 million. According to statistics provided by the government, 97 percent of the population is Muslim. Approximately 3 percent of the population is composed of Christians, Yezidis, Sabean-Mandae-ans, Bahais, Shabaks, Kaka'is (sometimes referred to as Ahl-e Haqq), and a very small number of Jews. Shia, although predominantly located in the south and east, are also a majority in Baghdad and have communities in most parts of the country. Sunnis form the majority in the west, center, and the north of the country.

Reported estimates from leaders of the Christian population in 2003 ranged from 800,000 to 1.4 million. Current population estimates by Christian leaders range from 400,000 to 600,000. Approximately two-thirds of Christians are Chaldeans (an eastern rite of the Catholic Church), nearly one-fifth are Assyrians (Church of the East), and the remainder are Syriacs (Eastern Orthodox), Armenians (Roman Catholic and Eastern Orthodox), Anglicans, and other Protestants. Most Assyrian Christians are in the north, and most Syriac Christians are split among the Baghdad, Kirkuk, and Ninewa Provinces. Christian leaders estimated that as much has [sic] 50 percent of the country's Christian population lives in Baghdad, and 30 to 40 percent lives in the north, with the largest Christian communities located in and around Mosul, Erbil, Dohuk, and Kirkuk. The archbishop of the Armenian Orthodox Diocese reported that 15,000 to 16,000 Armenian Christians remained in the country, primarily in the cities of Baghdad, Basrah, Kirkuk, and Mosul. Evangelical Christians reportedly number between 5,000 and 6,000. They can be found in the northern part of the country, as well as in Baghdad, with a small number residing in Basrah. Eight Jews reside in Baghdad, and none are known to live in other parts of the country.[13]

Although coalition forces pulled out of Iraq at the end of 2011, we cannot pull out our compassion and prayers for those who continue to suffer and die for their faith. Please keep this country's faithful in your heart and minds as you seek to fulfill God's purpose for your life.

With every knock on the door, Neha and her family feared they would be killed. They were branded by the Muslim extremists—labeled as Christians who had refused to convert to Islam. "I went to the police. I told them what happened, I told them how my family and I were being threatened…but they didn't listen to me," says Neha's father. Neha and her family had no choice but to pack up their few belongings and move to a small underground space with no windows, concrete walls with only a bed and chair.

7

AFRICA

The first time I heard Neha's story from her father and looked into her sad, big brown eyes, I knew I had to help her—I had to help the family escape from hiding, from living in constant fear. The tears in the eyes of her parents were heart wrenching. They were, after all, not murderers, not thieves, not criminals—they were Christians. As Neha's father told me about her nightmares, I remembered my own haunting nightmares—not so much my ordeal, but the screams I heard in the Egyptian prison of women being raped and men being tortured...and how helpless I felt that I could not go to their aid.

NIGERIA

VIOLENCE HAS ALSO OVERTAKEN CHRISTIANS in Nigeria where dozens were killed in several attacks by Muslim extremists on Christmas Eve and New Year's Eve 2011. These attacks included the Christmas Eve killing of a Baptist pastor in his home and some members of the congregation who were in an adjoining church that was set on fire, as well as several bomb attacks, including one in the nation's capital on New Year's Eve.

And in January 2012, at least 143 people were killed in coordinated attacks in Nigeria's largest city, Kano. A Boko Haram spokesman claimed responsibility for the attacks because the state government refused to release Boko Haram members held by the police. Boko Haram has carried out increasingly sophisticated and bloody attacks in its campaign to implement strict sharia law across Nigeria, a multiethnic nation of more than 160 million people. Boko Haram, whose name means "Western education is sacrilege" in the local language, is responsible for at least 510 killings in 2011, according to the Associated Press. Targets include both Muslims and Christians. However, Christians are specifically being targeted; the group promised to kill any Christians living in Nigeria's predominantly Muslim north. "That has further inflamed religious and ethnic tensions in Nigeria, which has seen ethnic violence kill thousands in recent years along the divide between the north and the largely Christian south."[1]

SUDAN

Also in January 2012, police in Sudan arrested and beat James Kat of the Evangelical Church of Sudan. The action was believed to be in response to a letter to the Sudanese Presbyterian Evangelical Church leaders from Sudan's Ministry of Guidance and Religious Endowments that threatened to arrest pastors if they were caught evangelizing or failed to provide their names and contact information. Under the majority Muslim country's Interim National Constitution, shar'ia is a source of legislation and the laws and policies of its government also favor Islam, according to the U.S. State Department's latest International Religious Freedom Report.

According to reports, in a related incident, a church leader was arrested after he refused to be evicted. Freed on bail, the pastor fears being arrested again as police continue to threaten him and his family. Police began demolishing the church compound fence. "They will definitely demolish my house," the pastor said. "I am in great terror; I'm afraid to sleep in the house, because

100

they may come again and arrest me. This is a clear form of terrorism against Christians."

"Many other Christians face persecution from Muslim communities and their government representatives, both of whom want to rid Sudan of Christianity. Many claim that Christianity is now treated as an alien religion following the departure of 350,000 Sudanese—most of them Christians—to South Sudan after the secession," reported Joseph DeCaro for *Worthy News* in January 2012.[2] Those who remain, approximately 500,000 of southern ethnic origin, fear that they will be forced to submit to Shariah law or leave, overwhelming the fledgling South Sudan and causing yet another refugee crisis in the region. Yet no one is talking about the situation. Do we need another Darfur before the world wakes up?

Nigeria and Sudan have both been a focus of my work through OFWI and in the case of the Sudan even before I fled Egypt. We have recently helped refugees from the Sudan start a new life in Canada and closely monitor the situation in Nigeria and other countries. I could fill an entire book with all of the atrocities against Christians that occur regularly in various African countries. Suffice it to say that it is our responsibility to at the very least pray for the safety and peace of those living on that troubled continent.

———◄O►———

When we met Reverend Majed El Shafie and he told us that it was possible to escape Pakistan and that we could live without fear, I thanked God for that little seed of an answer to my aching prayers. My family and I waited and waited, month after month, we moved from safehouse to safehouse—strengthened now with the hope that we might finally rest peacefully at night and during the day not have to cower with each knock on the door.

8

PAKISTAN

In 2004, I established One Free World International to help Neha and her family and others like them. I peaceably but forcibly fought governments day after day for three and a half years to bring Neha's family to freedom, just as I promised her. There were times when I woke in the night and prayed, "God, why did You put me in this position...why did You give me this heavy burden?" I would almost give up hope when things didn't work out, thinking what can a little guy like me do about these life-and-death situations. Then came morning and it was a new day. I would get dressed, tie my shoes, and say, "Maybe I'm not doing everything—but I will do something!"

IN APRIL 2009, I LED a delegation of North American politicians and religious leaders to Pakistan for high-level meetings with Pakistani officials to discuss human rights issues and confront them with evidence of abuses in their country. This was a tremendous opportunity for One Free World International to affect real change in Pakistan on behalf of religious minorities and oppressed and exploited women and children.

This mission was the result of almost four years of hard work, involving several trips to Pakistan and presenting evidence to the Canadian parliamentary Sub-Committee on Human Rights.

After we finally persuaded the Pakistani government to meet with us, they still tried to cancel our meetings at the last minute, but our persistence finally paid off.

Our delegation met with the Cabinet Ministers responsible for Foreign Affairs, Human Rights, and Minority Affairs. During tense meetings overshadowed by security concerns, I strongly denounced Pakistan's Blasphemy Laws. These vague and draconian laws are used by Muslim extremists to intimidate and oppress religious minorities and to settle personal scores and petty disputes with minorities or among Muslims, ruining the lives of entire families—and often resulting in the death of the victim.

We also demanded authorities protect minority girls and prosecute those who rape and forcibly convert them to Islam. I presented evidence obtained by OFWI of labor camps where Christians and other minorities live and work as modern-day slaves in appalling conditions and discussed human trafficking, which is a serious related problem in Pakistan.

In the presence of our delegation, including a member of parliament, church leaders, and a media professional, the Pakistani officials admitted they could not deny our evidence. They promised to work toward shutting down the slave camps and invited me to return to revisit the issue. In the meantime, I informed the Pakistani officials that we would be urging the Canadian government to link our development aid to improvements in these areas. Also discussed at length was the situation of minorities in the Swat Valley, where the government had entered into a peace agreement with the Taliban extremist group and where all-out war has since broken out between government forces and the Taliban.

BLASPHEMY LAWS

Foremost among official measures reinforcing the persecution of minorities in Pakistan are the Blasphemy Laws which were enacted in their current form in the early to mid-1980s.

Furthermore, as recently as May 2007, Muslim parties put forward a bill called *The Apostasy Act 2006*, which proposed death for males and life imprisonment for females who change their religion from Islam. Although the bill has not been officially passed into law, the government did not oppose it, but rather sent it to a parliamentary committee for consideration. Intentionally or not, this grants the principles espoused in the apostasy bill and in the Blasphemy Laws an air of credence and legitimacy, reinforces the second-class citizenship and endangers the lives of minorities and converts.

Despite repeated promises by past regimes that they would be repealed, the vague and draconian Blasphemy Laws remain in force and very much in use. Far from being merely a symbolic and irrelevant gesture, the blasphemy provisions are still a powerful tool in the hands of Islamic extremists—so much so that vocal opponents of these laws have paid with their lives, including two prominent politicians as mentioned in an article I have cited below.

These blasphemy provisions, contained in sections 295B-C of the Pakistani Penal Code (along with sections 298 A-C that specifically target Ahmadis), mandate life imprisonment for defiling, damaging, or desecrating a copy of the Koran or an extract from it and life imprisonment or death for derogatory remarks, direct or indirect, against the Islamic prophet Mohammed. The Blasphemy Laws are primarily used to terrorize minorities and pursue personal scores and vendettas. While they are commonly used to pursue disputes among Muslims, religious minorities are particularly vulnerable to their use and their very existence undermines any effective freedom of religion in Pakistan. The definition of "blasphemy" is so broad and vague that it constitutes an affront to any conceivable notion of the rule of law and international human rights standards. An individual can easily breach this law without intention and almost any comment or gesture can be interpreted as a violation at the accuser's whim and fancy.

The potentially unlimited scope of the "crime" of "blasphemy" is illustrated by section 295C, which reads:

> 295-C. Use of derogatory remarks, etc., in respect of the Holy Prophet: Whoever by words, either spoken or written, or by visible representation or by *any imputation, innuendo, or insinuation, directly or indirectly,* defiles the sacred name of the Holy Prophet Muhammad (peace be upon him) shall be punished with death, or imprisonment for life, and shall also be liable to fine[1] (emphasis added).

Intimidation and threats against lawyers and judges makes defending against blasphemy charges difficult; nevertheless, the death sentence is usually overturned on appeal. However, even when the conviction or sentence is reversed, the accused has typically spent several years in prison on false charges in dreadful conditions, facing daily abuse from guards and fellow inmates. Numerous accused who were acquitted by the courts have been killed by mobs or Muslim vigilantes on their release. Others have been killed by Muslim prisoners while awaiting a verdict in their case.

One of the cases we have been following and advocated on behalf of is that of Asia Bibi (also known as Asia Noreen) who remains in prison under a death sentence for "blasphemy." She had been targeted by Muslim women in her village and pressured several times to convert to Islam. When she refused, the village women provoked a confrontation. Asia had obliged one of the women by bringing her water at her request; but when she did so, the other women made statements accompanied by insults that Muslims could not drink water provided by a non-Muslim. Asia replied by questioning the women whether all people are not human beings and an argument ensued during which she stated her conviction that Jesus, not Mohammed is the true prophet.

Not long after, a mob of village Muslims led by a local cleric attacked Asia. She was saved by police who took her to the police station where they charged her with blasphemy on the basis of a complaint by the cleric. The lawyers working on her appeal have been subject to death threats, and Asia herself has been repeatedly beaten and mistreated by Muslim prison guards.

Another case that illustrates the senselessness and danger of the Blasphemy Laws is that of Jagdeesh Kumar, a young Hindu factory worker in Karachi, who was accused of blasphemy and beaten to death by his Muslim co-workers in one spontaneous mob incident in April 2008. These laws are dangerous and must be repealed; and on behalf of Pakistani minorities, we must do everything in our power to encourage the Pakistani authorities to do so.

GHETTOS AND SLAVE CAMPS

Charles Colony is typical of the living situation facing minorities in many areas of Pakistan. The typical Christian community here consists of "houses" that are actually holes dug in the ground with bricks—no mortar—stacked around the hole on three sides with a ragged old tarp as a roof for protection from rain, heat, debris. The only water—stagnant—is held in a dirty cement trough that serves about 100 families. There is no food, no clean water, no school for the children—no dignity. And the only reason for these conditions—the families are Christians.

Besides Charles Colony, we also visited one of the brick factories where Christians, Sikhs, and Hindus lived—lived and worked as slaves making bricks. The only way out of these modern-day slave camps is to convert to Islam or sell a kidney. We met with Saleem Khokar, a member of Parliament Sindh Assembly of Pakistan, and he confirmed that the only way out of the forced labor camps is to convert or to sell a kidney. And if a person is caught trying to escape, some of their fingers would be chopped off. We spoke to a

5-year-old boy who receives only one meal a day and is given only 2-3 drinks of water a day.

At a small colony that OFWI established for slaves who have been freed, we spoke to a group who were eager to tell us about their treatment in the slave camp and show us the scars on their legs where the chains had dug into their flesh. A little boy told us that he saw his parents being beaten. He didn't know how old he was but he thought "about 13 or 14"—he had never attended school. Instead, he worked in the fields day after day after day.

Before leaving Pakistan, the delegation met with leaders of Pakistani religious minorities and held a press conference during which I criticized the Pakistani press for failing to address these issues. "In Pakistan there is a serious violation of human rights against the minorities," I told the media. "We will stand with the minorities. We are not leaving one soul behind. The only way to get out of this issue is by killing me because I'm not going anywhere."

Although we were pleased to have been able to have these discussions, OFWI continues to keep pressure on the Pakistani government to ensure concrete results. We will not let up until we have proof that the Pakistani government has indeed taken effective measures to protect the country's minorities.

PAKISTAN'S FLOOD

I have no doubt you remember the devastating flood in Pakistan in 2010 that killed about 2,000 people and left 11 million homeless. But do you remember hearing about how financial aid from other countries was used to persecute minorities and force conversions to Islam?

Millions saw their homes and livelihoods destroyed and were faced with the threat of infectious diseases in relief camps and affected areas. Foreign governments provided official aid, and Canadians and Americans opened their hearts and donated generously through various humanitarian organizations to assist the victims of the flood. What you did not hear about are the silent victims of that disaster—those whose lives were shattered by the natural disaster and who have since been denied assistance in a man-made disaster-in-the-making.

It came to OFWI's attention through our sources in Pakistan that in some hard-hit areas, including parts of the Swat Valley and Sindh province, minorities including Christians, Hindus, and Ahmadiyya Muslims were refused aid because of their religion. Rescuers passed over minorities leaving them to fend for themselves. Local workers and government officials distributed international aid to Muslims but denied aid to religious minorities or turned them away at relief camps. Some were told to convert to Islam to access aid. Because of the desperate situation, some non-Muslims chose to lie and claim they were Muslim so their families would have a chance at survival.

The experience of one Hindu community of 19 families in a village near Taunsa Barrage illustrates what took place among Christians, Hindus, and other minorities in some of the affected flooded areas. The community was forced to rescue their livestock and families themselves when rescue teams did not help after their mud homes were flattened by floodwaters. They were not allowed in the relief camp because they were not Muslim, but when they sought to have food aid delivered to them at their location outside the camp, they were told they had to come to the camp to receive their aid. Yet due to their distance from the camp and prevailing flood-related conditions, they were unable to make the necessary several daily treks to the camp.

This was a terrible abuse of vulnerable victims and a gross violation of their dignity and human rights. Moreover, it sets the stage for future abuses when individuals seek to reclaim their former lives and religious identities after having given in to pressure to convert or pass themselves off as Muslim in order to gain access to aid to which they ought to have a right. In a country where apostasy from and claims of blasphemy against Islam can lead to death, these unfortunate people who only wanted food for their families on an equal basis with other flood victims were forced to face an uncertain and dangerous future—and an added threat that their Muslim neighbors never faced.

As the world moved its attention to other issues and as Pakistan moved from relief to rebuilding, we vowed not to leave behind those who have no voice. Our governments must demand that our aid be distributed to those who need it—without regard to religious or other criteria. If these basic requirements are not met, we must stop all aid immediately. There is no excuse to justify giving aid only to a certain segment of the population whether it is on religious or any other grounds.

Under no circumstances should our governments condone such action by continuing to give aid that may be used to force people to convert to Islam. This is particularly important in the rebuilding stage as the decisions made today will have far-reaching and even permanent effects. We must not allow natural disasters to be used to further oppress and devastate the downtrodden minorities of Pakistan.

TERRORISM

For years Pakistan has played an important role on the international stage because of its strategic location. Western countries have ignored its ofttimes complacent attitude when it comes to terrorists within its borders. Yet Pakistan's commitment to international interests in the region and to international human rights standards in general and, as already seen above, to religious freedom in particular, is suspect at best. This outlook was confirmed in 2002 when Daniel Pearl, an American journalist, was kidnapped in Karachi and beheaded after he was forced to profess that he was an American Jew, his parents were Jews, and that he practiced Judaism. It came full circle and was confirmed with the discovery in 2011 of Osama Bin Laden's hiding place only miles from a major state military academy and installation.

The following article about Pakistan is relevant in its frank explanation of the atmosphere surrounding the country's current hard-to-ignore disregard for religious liberty.

> But it is Pakistan, perhaps America's most obvious "frenemy," [friend-enemy] that best illustrates why religious persecution is a problem transcending national boundaries. Freedom of conscience, the essence of religious liberty, is a foundation for all other human rights.
>
> A national community that refuses to even accept, let alone defend, those who believe differently is likely to become a source of intolerance, hatred, and violence—which may end up directed well beyond its own country's boundaries. A government unwilling to protect individuals worshiping and serving their creator, both singly and collectively, is not likely to respect the life, dignity, and freedom of its citizens, and even less so people from other nations. Such a regime certainly will find itself ill-equipped to confront the very extremist forces it has previously, even if inadvertently, encouraged.
>
> The ongoing disintegration of Pakistani society was dramatically illustrated by the assassinations of Punjab governor Salman Taseer in January [2011] and Religious Minorities minister Shahbaz Bhatti in March [2011]. Taseer was a Muslim who opposed the religious parties and denounced Pakistan's blasphemy law. Bhatti, known internationally, also opposed the blasphemy laws and said he was "speaking for the oppressed, marginalized and persecuted Christians

and other minorities." Although a few brave Pakistanis embraced the two men in death, many more, including in Taseer's own ruling Pakistan People's Party, stayed silent while extremists praised the murderers.

In such an environment, it should surprise no one to find official support for al-Qaeda and other terrorists. While civilian members of the Pakistani government may have had no idea about Osama bin Laden's presence on Pakistani soil, it beggars belief that members of the military and Inter-Services Intelligence (ISI) agency did not know, and did not aid him. A poll last year found that some 60 percent of Pakistanis viewed America as an enemy. Rank-and-file military attitudes seem little different.[2]

In August 2009, a Christian family of seven, including two children, was burned alive by Muslim extremists. They locked the doors from the outside and set the home on fire. Is that justice? Is that good? What kind of god condones such action? We visited Pakistan shortly afterward to see the damage for ourselves. It was still dangerous, with smaller, isolated attacks ongoing, leaving us on edge whether we would be attacked while we were there. Emotions continued to run high and it was difficult to observe the pain and destruction.

We visited Korian and Gojra, two predominantly Christian towns near the Pakistani city of Faisalabad. False accusations that a copy of the Koran had been defiled during a Christian wedding had spread quickly through the countryside. A few days later, on July 30, 2009, Korian was attacked and some 60 houses burned. The following day the mosques in four Muslim towns which surround the village of Gojra openly declared jihad against the Christians, leading to the August 1, 2009, attack on Gojra, a village of 3,000 Christians and other minorities, by a mob of 10,000 Muslims armed with machetes, machine guns, and Molotov cocktails. Despite being fully on notice of the impending attacks, 300 government security personnel did nothing to protect the village. Many just stood and watched while some fled and others even encouraged the attackers. The Muslim mob blocked roads to prevent the arrival of fire rescue crews while a church and some 50 houses were burned to the ground, including the house mentioned in which the family had been burned alive.

I stood in the charred empty cement shell of that small, once-humble home, shocked yet again at the cruelty human beings can visit on other human beings. The blackened walls told a story too horrible to comprehend. I flew home from this mission with a heavy heart and a suitcase packed with the remains of a Bible that had been burned and some of the charred clothing the father had been wearing when the family had been burned alive.

Hearing about events such as these is certainly shocking, but it is far too easy to dismiss mere words. Standing at the actual scene, touching the charred remains of items these victims held dear and knowing they will never turn the pages of that Bible again—slaughtered as less than animals simply because they were Christians—the experience touches a place deep in your soul and alters your perspective on life. It speaks of truth and justice, of humanity and the desperate need to continue the fight for a world where every man, woman, and child has the freedom to pursue the meaning of life on his or her own terms.

In December 2009, three and a half years after first hearing about Neha, her rescue was imminent. I went to Pakistan with only one camera man, my producer Chris Atkins. I felt a heavy burden for him as this was a dangerous mission and he had a wife and two children. I feared for his life. I also felt the weight of Neha and her family upon me—as they, too, may be killed during the rescue attempt. When I met with the Pakistani officials and gave them the bribe money they demanded, they wanted more. I had no more to give them. "Please give me the family and after we are back in Canada, I will send you more money," I pleaded.

Finally I was able to go to the Canadian embassy to retrieve the family's passports containing their precious visas—the documents were ready for me and I thanked God that part of the plan was successful. The night before our flight to Canada, I went to the family's hiding place—the underground room where all seven members lived.

"Tomorrow we are taking you to Canada and this will be the land of your freedom for you and your family," I told them. I could see the fear in their eyes and at the same time the hope. As I looked into Neha's eyes and those of her brothers and sister, all I could think about was how I could lose all of them if I made one mistake.

Very early in the morning, while still dark, all nine of us squeezed into two cars and started driving toward the airport. We passed by many security checkpoints without any trouble. We praised God! When we arrived at the airport and walked inside, and as I was handing the security guard the passports, I knew that God didn't bring us all this way over the past few years to fail us now. I knew that if God remembers every bird in every tree, every fish in every ocean, every little ant under every little rock, surely He would remember me and my promise to Neha.

When we arrived in Canada, Neha and her family were greeted at the airport with flowers and flags and cheering people, welcomed with open arms by members of the local Pakistani Christian community and friends of OFWI who had supported the family and our mission for four long years.

I smiled to myself and sighed as a sense of relief that I had not felt since I learned about little Neha invaded my being. "Mission accomplished!"

IN THE NEWS

Our daring mission had a happy ending, for which we all thanked God. Canadian media wrote and broadcast our story, which made it even more meaningful as more and more people worldwide became aware of the plight of so many persecuted Christians in Pakistan and other countries. The following excerpt is part of an especially poignant report about the mission by a Canadian television news magazine, W5:

> Majed El Shafie founded One Free World International as a human rights organization to help persecuted minorities. He too was persecuted in his native Egypt after he embraced Christianity and began an underground movement. He claims that he was arrested and jailed for agitating for Christians. He showed W5 scars on his back that he says he received after being tortured in prison. Within a year he fled Egypt and found his way to Canada in 2002. Two years later, he started OFWI.
>
> El Shafie learned of Neha's plight from contacts within the Pakistani-Canadian community and decided he had to help the little girl and her family. What began was years of lobbying, trips to Pakistan and subterfuge to bring the Masih family to Canada.

"I gave her my word and my promise that I would get her out of there," El Shafie said, recalling his first meeting with Neha and her family.

One of the main hurdles El Shafie faced was obtaining Canadian immigration documents that would allow Neha and her family to come to Canada. Luckily, he had an important contact: Canada's Minister of Immigration, Jason Kenney, whom he had worked with on other human rights cases.

The details of the Masih family's ordeal compelled Kenney to do something that he has only done twice before, personally issuing the family a special Temporary Resident Permit to guarantee they could enter Canada and eventually apply for permanent residence.

"We can't go into every country in the world, in every unjust situation and sort of, metaphorically speaking, airlift people to Canada," Kenney told W5, as he stressed that the special immigration papers had been issued due to the uniqueness of the Masih family's situation.

"When you see a girl who has suffered what she did, when you see a family that lost all of its sense of hope and dignity, I just felt absolutely compelled to do whatever we could to help them."

ESCAPE

With Kenney's help and the Canadian government opening its doors, El Shafie returned to Pakistan to help the Masih family escape. Fearing attack or reprisal, El Shafie says he had to obtain the family's Pakistani passports through backdoor channels and on the pretence that they would return to Pakistan after a short visit to Canada.

Even the trip to the airport in Islamabad was fraught with danger. Still under threat of death, and aided by El Shafie, Neha's family quietly slipped into the international air terminal and boarded a flight to Toronto. Only once the plane had reached cruising altitude and had left Pakistani airspace could they breathe a sigh of relief. Fifteen hours later they arrived at Toronto's Pearson airport to the delight and applause of Canadian Christians, many of whom assisted in the rescue by offering financial donations to help pay for the trip.

The family is now safe in Canada but the situation in Pakistan remains tense. Recently, as Pakistan has become embroiled in the war against terror—pitting pro-Taliban elements against the government—minorities have been targeted as allies of the West and, in particular, the United States.

"This is a country which is at war with religious extremism," said Sahebzada Khan, Pakistan's Consul General in Toronto, who acknowledges his country faces a serious problem. "These religious extremists are not just killing minorities, they are killing our way of life."[3]

9

MAKING A DIFFERENCE

I FOUNDED ONE FREE WORLD International (OFWI) in 2004 because I wanted to make a positive difference in the lives of those suffering for their faith. After experiencing firsthand the horror of torture and knowing that thousands and millions of others were in the same or much worse situations compelled me to take action.

OFWI is an international human rights organization based in Toronto, Canada, that focuses on the rights of religious minorities around the world and promotes tolerance, understanding, and respect for diverse religious beliefs.

OFWI's goal is a world in which people are free to choose, retain, change, and express their religious or nonreligious belief system in accordance with their conscience, without fear and with full equality and dignity, while fully respecting the corresponding rights of others.

Our primary focus is on combating the persecution of Christians and anti-Semitism, and we assist all those whose religious freedom is threatened, regardless of their beliefs. OFWI is based on and guided in its work by Christian principles. It does not endorse the religious beliefs of those on behalf of whom it advocates, but is

119

uncompromising about promoting their right to hold and exercise those beliefs.

OFWI believes that, along with the right to life, religious freedom and freedom of conscience are the first and most fundamental of human rights. The ability to believe (or to choose not to believe) in something beyond our material existence, in accordance with our individual conscience, and to manifest that belief in practices and observances is one of the most essential distinguishing characteristics of the human race. Thus, persecution of people for their beliefs or coercing others into adopting, changing, or denying their beliefs denies the very humanity of the person who is thus violated.

PROMOTING AWARENESS

As a result, OFWI promotes awareness of human rights abuses and comes to the aid of those who are suffering because of their religious beliefs or expression. OFWI's activities include advocacy, awareness campaigns, seminars, research, fact-finding, expert testimony, and practical assistance, among others. We encourage all people who believe in basic human freedoms to join us in our worldwide efforts to aid those who are suffering. Your God-given talents, gifts, and skills can make a positive difference when channeled in ways that bring hope, comfort, and peace.

OFWI advocates on behalf of religious freedom before governments, courts, and international and multinational human rights bodies. It also pursues dialogue with government officials and policymakers with the aim of promoting changes in policy toward violators to ensure that they will not be able to enjoy impunity for their actions.

One Free World International is a voice for the voiceless to ensure that justice will prevail and the dream of a world where all are free and equal would be realized. Please consider adding your voice to ours. We have provided some suggestions below.

RELIGIOUS PERSECUTION REFUGEES

Religious persecution is a growing cause of refugees around the world today and refugee policy is an important part of all countries with humane values and a sense of responsibility within the broader world community. While these provisions are open to abuse, we must not forget that peoples' lives are in the balance and means must be found to keep those people who do not have legitimate claims from entering—and to allow those who do to enter into safety. Aside from helping the obvious life-saving assistance to persecuted refugees themselves, accepting refugees from persecution is also another way in which countries can send an important message to persecuting states about their behavior. Yet all too often legitimate refugees, and especially those fleeing religious persecution, get left out in the dangerous cold.

As religious extremism spreads, all countries with humane consciences must be prepared with an appropriate response. Currently, Canadian, United States, and most European immigration and refugee policies do not address the issues adequately.

Serious reform is needed on both procedural and substantive fronts. To reform refugee procedure, we must:

- ensure that we appoint qualified decision makers;

- ensure that decision makers are unbiased both in fact and appearance; and,

- allow claimants a reasonable opportunity to present evidence, make their claim, and to be represented by competent counsel and other technical assistance (e.g., translators) of their choosing.

- With regard to the substance of refugee claims and how they are assessed, we must:

- educate decision makers about the existence and dynamics of religious persecution;

- revise the presumptions of state protection and internal relocation; and,

- approach the credibility of claimants in light of the cultural context.

A most worrisome trend is the comments that we have seen from decision makers regarding the credibility of claimants, comments that do not even fit our Western worldview. Some of the comments would at the very least be questionable if they were made in the context of a domestic case involving spousal, child, or sexual abuse, bullying, organized crime, or gang violence. We have learned enough about the psychology and dynamics of these situations that certain actions on the part of the victim or perpetrator that otherwise seem illogical or irrational are understandable within the context. Victims of religious persecution, on the other hand, are judged to a different standard, yet religious persecution closely resembles the cases of bullying and organized crime or gang violence, etc., and we must not consider incredible in one case that which is accepted as credible in the other.

Judges have rejected the credibility of claimants for various reasons, including for example the lack of a prolonged history of abuse, a lack of subjective fear indicated by the claimant's temporary return to their country or by the claimant's stay in a first country of refuge beyond a negative refugee determination (effectively resulting in the bizarre situation that the claimant might not be believed regardless of whether they leave or stay), because the alleged persecutors were "unknown colleagues," and because the claimant had not reported an incident to authorities, for example, police or university officials. In some cases judges appear to require the claimant to have actually done what their persecutors accused them of even though the persecutors cared only that the claimant was stated to have, for example, assisted someone in converting, regardless of whether they actually had done so or not.

A judge looking through a Western paradigm cannot see the circumstances the claimant was coping with and can only see contradictory evidence which leads them to determine a lack of credibility. For example, in one case of a Christian whose claim was based on a fear of persecution and torture because he was married to a Muslim and who traveled on a passport stating he was Muslim (in his explanation to "avoid problems"), the judge stated that the lack of a marriage certificate indicating the claimant's religion as Christian was evidence of his lack of credibility. Without commenting on the rest of the claim, clearly the unavailability of the marriage certificate was irrelevant in this case. If a non-Muslim man was travelling on a Muslim passport to avoid problems because of his association with a Muslim woman, he could hardly be expected to give his religion as anything other than Muslim, regardless of his true beliefs, on the very marriage certificate that would effectively be his death warrant. Yet a judge viewing this from a Western perspective cannot understand this kind of behavior and interprets the inconsistency as a lack of credibility; yet by its very adverse inference it may in fact support the credibility of the claimant. All of these arguments by incredulous Western judges betray a lack of understanding and education about the cultural context of religious persecution or an unwillingness to accept that a problem exists.

ARMED WITH KNOWLEDGE

The point of refugee protection is to provide asylum for refugees when there is sufficient evidence that the person has a well-founded fear of persecution or cruel and unusual treatment, including the possibility of torture and risk to life. Where there are sufficient grounds for fear, we cannot afford to wait for the danger to materialize or for evidence of "a prolonged history of abuse" before we step in to help nor can we eliminate refugees, religious persecution, or the problem of Islamist violence or state-sponsored religious coercion by pretending that they do not exist.

We have allowed Muslim extremists and terrorists, such as Ramzi Youssef, one of the masterminds of the 1993 World Trade Center bombing, to use our refugee determination system in order to gain access to our soil. How much more must we help those innocent people whose only crime is to follow a religion that is not approved by their state or accepted by their fellow countrymen and who will reward our compassion with their undying loyalty, support, and cooperation?

During the Nazi holocaust, many Western countries including Canada and the United States had severely restrictive immigration policies that prevented thousands of Jews from immigrating to safety. Rather than face the reality of what was happening in Europe and do something to help, Canada and the United States preferred to send back Jewish refugees, like those who arrived on the *St. Louis*, and many died in Nazi death camps.

In the end, perhaps many allied soldiers who died fighting for the freedoms that we hold dear could have been spared if we had confronted the problem appropriately in the first place by standing up for truth and freedom. The price of ignoring the problem is too high. We must communicate clearly to violator states that their behavior is unacceptable and revise our respective refugee policies to deal appropriately with those seeking refuge from religious persecution.

WHAT YOU CAN DO

Religious persecution worldwide is an ocean of evil that is impossible for one person to fight alone. Together, however, we can accomplish great things. You can get involved in helping change the worldview of people and nations in several practical and important ways:

1. Become familiar with and stay current with issues regarding religious persecution. Because this life and death problem plagues the world, perhaps you may

[handwritten margin note: Even after the war, restrictions on Jewish immigration continued in the US and many other places. Israel was the only safe place many Holocaust survivors could reach.]

want to choose a certain country, region, or city where people are suffering for their faith to follow in detail. Find out all you can about these places and people. Although some injustices have been exposed in this book, I hope the information has piqued your interest and stirred your desire to delve more deeply. There are many reliable websites that post updates regarding places and people who are targets of zealots or harsh governmental sanctions against them. Educating yourself about and becoming more aware of people of faith opens a world that you will quickly realize needs your help. OFWI posts alerts on its website (www.one-freeworldinternational.org) with specific concerns and prayer requests and it is a good place to start.

2. Prayer is one of the most crucial ways to help—anyone anywhere. When you pray for people, God's heart opens and situations positively change. Prayer links all believers in a way that evil cannot penetrate—in ways that overcome the circumstances. OWFI urges you to pray for those you know and those you don't know who are suffering because of their faith. I suggest that you choose a particular time of day and dedicate those moments, for example the five minutes you spend with your morning cup of coffee, in concentrated prayer for people who are being abused because their beliefs or religious practices do not conform with those around them. You may want to form a prayer group devoted to gathering and praying once a week for the concerns and requests posted on the OFWI website, or requests presented by your church or a missionary organization. Any and every intimate prayer you share with God will not go unanswered. He is faithful in all ways.

3. Contacting government officials and politicians makes a tangible difference. Because your vote and your voice

count during elections, a letter or phone call from you is heard. You may have doubts about how seriously your concerns are taken by elected officials, but it is vital that we don't silence ourselves because of doubt. I have spoken to many holding political office, and they assure me that every constituent's contact with their office is regarded as important. Moreover, these days it is easy to reach an official as each has a website that lists their email address, their mailing address, and their phone number so that you can voice your opinion. When making contact, it is best if you voice clearly your concern and then follow up with your recommendation about how to rectify the problem. For instance, regarding China, you may want to state the human and religious rights violations and then suggest that your government tie trade relations with that country to improvement in its human rights record, conveying that you have personally chosen to boycott products from China.

4. Choosing to assist organizations like OFWI that work in this area with financial support is essential. Many are not aware of the need, but OFWI, for one, does not receive government funding or private foundation sponsorship nor is it supported by any denominational mission fund. Our work on behalf of the persecuted is supported entirely by donations from individual supporters like yourself and the need is great. Your donations not only assure OFWI or other organizations that they can keep fighting the good fight against evil, they also provide the essential resources the staff needs to do things like: travel to countries to help free the unjustly persecuted men, women, and children; keep families safe while they hide for their lives; hire legal representation for those who can't afford it;

maintain a website informing the world of the issues and of those in need; and a myriad of other expenses required to bring awareness, hope, and freedom to millions of people who cannot be helped without your generous support. Some countries like Canada and the United States allow a tax deduction for donating to some nonprofit, nongovernmental organizations; this incentive is usually stated on the organization's website. However, regardless of charitable status, all legitimate, credible organizations will use your financial support to directly help those in need, so be thorough in your investigation of groups or organizations asking for financial assistance.

5. During political campaigns, prior to local, state, or national elections, is a prime time for bringing religious persecution issues front and center. While politicians and would-be politicians vie for the spotlight during their campaigns, you can start a conversation about how the candidate feels about and would vote regarding religious persecution at home and abroad. Bringing attention to this issue is the first step in making more people aware of its seriousness and widespread horror. A candidate's response will be telling, as the person will sympathize, reject, or ignore your concerns— whichever, you will have made an impression on the candidate and all within earshot and gleaned vital information on how you should vote. Be aware that taking a public stand for a cause greater than yourself is not only worthy of praise and admiration but it is also ridiculed and mocked. Knowing how God feels about the persecuted will give you the strength and conviction to do what is right, at the right time, and with the right attitude. Remember that Jesus said,

"Blessed are those who are persecuted because of righteousness,
for theirs is the kingdom of heaven" (Matthew 5:10).

———◄o►———

Despite the persecution, Christians are still victorious. The perse-cuted Christians are dying, but they are still smiling. They are in a very deep, dark night, but they still have the candle of the Lord, the candle of hope. Our enemy has a very strong weapon. Our enemy has a very strong army, but we have the Lord Almighty. Count on Him. We will fight unto the end in Jesus' name; and always remember, they can always kill the dreamer but no one can kill the dream.

EPILOGUE

Neha and her family have escaped persecution, violence, and death threats. One Sunday morning they attended church at the Toronto Airport Christian Fellowship, and were welcomed by their newfound Canadian Christian family, many of whom helped finance their subsistence over several years in hiding and their eventual rescue and escape. Neha and her family have embraced their new lives in Canada, where they practice their religion without fear of persecution or retaliation. Neha is attending school, speaks English fluently, and is enjoying getting to know and play with lots of children her age for the first time in her life. She tells me she is looking forward to being a human rights lawyer when she grows up.

I continue to be passionately involved with religious freedom advocacy, rescue missions, and humanitarian aid issues. We look forward to expanding our existing network of local sources beyond our current 28 countries while we continue to build bridges with governments in the free world and hope to expand our network and partnerships in Europe and Australia. I had the opportunity to testify about religious freedom issues once again before the Canadian Parliament and, for the first time, twice before the

United States Congress. I also recently organized and led the first Canadian delegation to visit Washington, DC, for the exclusive purpose of discussing human rights and freedom of religion around the world with American political leaders.

OFWI continues to bring hope to the slaves in Pakistan by buying freedom for as many as we can, and also by helping those who remain in the camps by providing them with food and clean water. We continue to monitor events in countries around the world and organize campaigns on behalf of individuals as well as highlighting specific incidents and broader situations. As I write these words, we are in the process of planning another highly sensitive rescue mission.

My documentary film *Freedom Fighter,* to which this book is the companion volume, has won numerous awards in the documentary film category at film festivals across North America. I have begun working on *Freedom Fighter II,* which highlights our ongoing efforts to bring to fruition one free world where people of all faiths can live without fear that they will be targeted for their beliefs.

My goal is to make the persecution of Christians not just a church or Christian matter, but an unavoidable human rights issue that concerns everyone who has a caring and compassionate heart. I want to unite oppressed minorities the world over—from every Christian denomination to Jews and any other minorities—to stand together and accomplish two things: first of all, to confront as many repressive or complicit regimes as possible with the immorality of their actions and stimulate positive changes in their treatment of their minorities. Second, I want to awaken the complacent or indifferent governments in the free world to recognize the fact and reality of persecution and to take up the challenge to pursue respect for the human rights of religious minorities around the world. In the process I want to show the love of Christ in action and share the good news that there is hope, forgiveness, and peace in the Prince of Peace for whoever chooses to accept it.

Appendix A

PRAYER AND ACTION REQUESTS

ONE FREE WORLD INTERNATIONAL PERIODICALLY posts prayer and action requests on our website to give visitors an opportunity to help us turn the tide of persecution worldwide with respect to individual victims or specific incidents. The following are some general suggestions for how you can pray about these issues. Then put your faith into action by taking the steps suggested.

Thank you for your response to those whose cries you may never hear in person, but who are nevertheless calling out to their brothers and sisters in every country, in every church, in every synagogue or temple of every name, and in every home. They are calling to you and to anyone who will listen, asking that you stand with them to help them live and worship without fear, but more than anything so that they can gain strength and courage from your support to face the trials that they must daily face.

WORLDWIDE PRAYER

Pray for those around the world who are persecuted for their faith or religious practices, that they would have strength, courage, and boldness to stand up for the truth and for justice regardless of the cost; pray also for miracles of protection that would strengthen their faith and cause their persecutors to turn their efforts toward seeking truth and justice; pray that those who are imprisoned and their families would find courage and comfort in their tribulations; pray that the more they are persecuted, the more they may seek God and grow in their knowledge and trust of Him. *"We are hard-pressed on every side, yet not crushed; we are perplexed, but not in despair; persecuted, but not forsaken; struck down, but not destroyed"* (2 Corinthians 4:8-9).

Pray for the persecutors—that, through witnessing Christ in the lives of those they are persecuting, they may turn to seeking peace and forgiveness; pray that they might come to know true peace through the Prince of Peace and in turn apply their energies toward spreading peace instead of hatred. *"And they overcame him by the blood of the Lamb and by the word of their testimony, and they did not love their lives to the death"* (Revelation 12:11).

Pray for government authorities that they would have the courage to govern their country with truth, justice, and righteousness, and to guarantee their people the freedom to seek and worship God in freedom and in accordance with their conscience and the wisdom to build up and strengthen their country by encouraging the active participation of religious minorities as full citizens. *"Therefore I exhort first of all that supplications, prayers, intercessions, and giving of thanks be made for all men, for kings and all who are in authority, that we may lead a quiet and peaceable life in all godliness and reverence"* (1 Timothy 2:1-2).

Pray that God would use the persecuted church to open the hearts of others to bring peace to the world for all people of faith; pray that the voice of the persecuted church will touch the hearts of the indifferent and bring them to an understanding that promotes freedom for all. *"that I may know Him and the power of His resurrection, and the fellowship of His sufferings, being conformed to His death"* (Philippians 3:10).

Pray for unity in the Body of Christ and between all those who are persecuted for their religious beliefs—that the plight of those persecuted for their faith will unify all churches and religions to work together for peace and justice for everyone. *"Behold, how good and how pleasant it is for brethren to dwell together in unity!"* (Psalm 133:1).

Pray for the governments of the United States, Canada, and the rest of the free world—that our leaders would open their hearts to the violation of Christians' and other religious minorities' rights in persecuted nations; pray that God would strengthen men and women of courage and integrity within our governments to stand firm and be bold in the fight against persecution worldwide. *"Righteousness exalts a nation, but sin is a reproach to any people"* (Proverbs 14:34).

Pray for forgiveness—that those who have experienced persecution will, through the grace of God, find the strength to *forgive* their persecutors and be released from the bondage of bitterness to victory through the power of forgiveness. *"For if you forgive men their trespasses, your heavenly Father will also forgive you"* (Matthew 6:14).

Pray for action—that people will become informed, that the truth will be revealed, that people will see the injustice and want to get involved and take action, and that God will grant each of us opportunities to make our voices heard. *"He has shown you, O man, what is good; and what does the Lord require of you but to do justly, to love mercy, and to walk humbly with your God?"* (Micah 6:8).

PRAYER FOR INDIVIDUAL COUNTRIES

Afghanistan

- pray for the secret Afghan Christians who have risked everything to follow their conscience by converting from Islam and embracing Christ;

- thank God for Said Musa, Shoaib Asadullah, and all those who have stood up for their faith even when doing so would cost them their liberty and possibly their life, and pray that their experiences will strengthen the faith of countless others; pray also for the safety of the families of those who remain in prison; and,

- pray for the people of Afghanistan, that they would experience true peace after decades of war and repression, and especially that they would have the courage to seek out truth, justice, and freedom for themselves and all Afghans.

China

- pray for the Chinese Christians and other religious minorities, that they would find opportunities in the midst of government control to follow their conscience in the pursuit of truth and greater meaning to life;

- pray for those imprisoned or constantly harassed by authorities that they would have peace and courage to endure their ordeal and to stand up for their beliefs and for the rights and freedoms of all Chinese citizens to worship freely; and,

- pray that the authorities would appreciate the virtue and benefits of recognizing and protecting the right of citizens to have freedom to worship and pursue religious knowledge and practices without being subject to control and enforced doctrines on the part of the authorities.

Egypt

- pray for safety and courage for the Christians and other religious minorities in Egypt, that they would stay strong and be protected from extremists trying to take advantage of opportunities in the political situation;

- pray for the people of Egypt and its leaders, that they would be able to take their country through an orderly and peaceful transition to freedom and a true democracy that respects the human rights of all Egyptians and that Muslim extremists would not be able to strengthen their positions; and,

- pray for Western and world leaders, that they would have the wisdom to respond appropriately to the turmoil and insecurity and maintain a strong stand for truth, peace, and human rights in Egypt.

Israel

- pray for miraculous protection and courage for the Arab Christians in the areas controlled by Hamas and the Palestinian Authority and that they would be a shining light in their communities of the love of Christ;

- pray for the Muslim extremists, that they would recognize the futility and evil of their persecution and oppression and turn their energies to seeking truth and justice; and,

- pray for safety and protection for Israel from attacks by terrorists within and hostile countries without where longstanding anti-Semitic sentiments have been reinforced as popular uprisings have spread and allowed extremists greater influence across the region.

Iran

- thank God for the courage of Christian converts like Maryam and Marzieh who were not afraid to stand up for their beliefs and for the truth regardless of the consequences and for bringing them to safety;

- pray for strength and courage for those like Pastor Nadarkhani who continue to face the prospect of the ultimate sacrifice for their beliefs and pray for protection and courage for their families;

- pray for the Iranian people that they would have the freedom to satisfy their thirst for truth and justice by exploring their religious beliefs and those of others around the world; and,

- pray that the authorities would stop their persecution of religious minorities, especially Christian converts and Bahai's, and grant them the freedom to pursue their religious beliefs and practices with full equality with their Muslim compatriots.

Iraq

- pray for the besieged Iraqi Christian community and other religious minorities, that they would remain strong, steadfast, and faithful in the midst of the great trials and dangers they face daily and that they and their homes would be miraculously protected from attacks; and,

- pray for the Iraqi people in general, that they would be able to put aside their differences and work together to rebuild their country after decades of war and oppression and that they would find true peace in the Prince of Peace.

Pakistan

- thank God for little Neha and pray for her physical and emotional healing and that her story would reach compassionate and fair-minded Pakistanis and serve to inspire positive changes in Pakistan;

- pray for the families of Korian and Gojra, that they would be filled with compassion and the love of Christ toward those who so brutally destroyed their homes, lives, and security, thus showing them a better way; and,

- pray for the repeal of the Blasphemy Laws and the closure of the slave camps and pray for protection and provision for poor religious minorities so that they would not feel the need to mortgage their lives just for the necessities of life.

PRAYER FOR ONE FREE WORLD INTERNATIONAL

- pray for One Free World International—that the team and our partners in our operations will receive continuing strength and courage to fight the good fight of faith;

- pray for opportunities and open doors at home and abroad that we might reach the halls of power with the need for action on behalf of religious minorities and respect for religious freedom;

- pray for wisdom and courage as we reach out to hostile nations and communities with the need to respect their minorities;

- pray especially for protection for the OFWI team as we continue to make interventions and, when necessary, undertake rescue missions in countries where the security situation is compromised; and,

- pray for faithful support and miraculous provision to enable us to do our work.

Action

As you know, the Bible teaches that faith without action is dead, so please take action and:

1. Become familiar and stay current with issues regarding religious persecution. Join OFWI's alert network (visit OFWI's website for more information) and follow the news both through traditional and cutting edge news sources like the internet and social media.

2. Write to governments that are oppressing their own citizens and express your concern over their actions, respectfully demanding that they protect and secure the internationally recognized human rights of minorities in their country. For some specific ideas you can see the suggestions we have provided at item 6 below. Advise them that you have been informed of the situation by One Free World International and that you will continue to monitor the situation in Pakistan and expect to see significant improvements in all of these areas and don't forget to send a copy of your correspondence to info@onefreeworldinternational.org for our records. Accurate contact information for virtually all officials can be found on the internet with a little searching and experience but if you are unable to find accurate information, do not hesitate to contact OFWI or the offices of your elected representatives to obtain up-to-date information.

3. Raise religious persecution as an issue during political campaigns at election time.

4. Contact your local member of parliament or representative to inform and educate them about what is happening to religious minorities around the world and to inquire what they have done through their position to protect religious minorities around the world.

5. Hold your government accountable for speaking out on behalf oppressed religious minorities, promoting respect for international human rights standards

and religious freedom, and for maintaining refugee policies that provide a real sanctuary for those who need emergency help. You can do this by writing to officials, especially your president or prime minister and the ministers or secretaries in charge of the relevant departments, including foreign affairs, refugee policy, international trade, and foreign aid. Ask them to respond to your letter and explain what your government has done on these issues and what results it has achieved or response it has received from countries of concern and don't forget to send a copy of your correspondence to OFWI at info@onefreeworldinternational.org. For some specific examples, see the suggestions provided at item 6.

6. Some specific suggestions for contacting government authorities:

Afghanistan

- write to the representative of Afghanistan in your country, demanding that the Afghan government repudiate its statements and repressive campaign against converts and repeal all apostasy laws releasing any converts immediately, and that it respect and promote international human rights standards and the rights of all Afghans to religious freedom; and,

- write to your government officials demanding that they honor the sacrifices made by our men and women who have made the ultimate sacrifice to bring truth, justice, and human rights to the people of Afghanistan by not resting until the Afghan government releases the prisoners who are held because of their faith and takes concrete measures toward ensuring true religious freedom for all Afghan citizens.

China

- join OFWI's boycott of Chinese products so that you can educate your friends and neighbors of the abuses taking place in China;

- write to the representative of China in your country and tell them that their control of religious expression by their citizens is immoral and that you will boycott China and spread the word of the government's abuses until you see concrete evidence that the government is taking effective measures to free religious prisoners and guarantee freedom of religious belief and expression;

- write to your government officials and demand that your government make human rights in China, and particularly religious freedom, a priority issue in its relations with China, including especially trade relations.

Egypt

- write to the representative of Egypt in your country demanding equal rights for religious minorities and respect for international human rights standards as well as respect for the peace treaty with Israel and the repudiation of anti-Semitic policies and incitement; and,

- write to your government officials urging them not to turn their attention away from Egypt and demanding that they push for the protection of Christians and other minorities and that they support only such processes and structures as respect human rights and the separation between religion and state as well as the peace between Egypt and Israel and more generally in the Middle East.

Iran

- write to the representative of Iran in your country demanding that they secure and enforce equal rights for religious minorities and especially that they stop their campaigns of harassment and persecution against Christian converts and Baha'is; and,

- write to your government officials urging them to use all means at their disposal to intervene on behalf of individuals targeted by the government for their beliefs and to promote respect for international human rights standards and religious freedom in Iran.

Iraq

- write to the representative of Iraq in your country demanding that the Iraqi government provide adequate protection and security for religious minorities and their property and that they take effective measures to secure and encourage respect for the rights of minorities; and,

- write to your government officials demanding that they use their influence with Iraqi officials to promote respect for the human rights of religious minorities.

Israel

- write to the representative of Israel in your country and assure them of your prayers and support for the security of Israel and its people; and,

- write to your government officials and urge them to support Israel's right to defend itself from attacks by anti-Semitic terrorists and hostile countries and to stand up for the rights of Christians in areas where they are in danger from Muslim extremists.

Pakistan

- write to the representative of Pakistan in your country demanding that the Pakistani government respect and uphold the human rights of its citizens and that it start by neutralizing and then repealing the Blasphemy Laws as well as shutting down the slave labor camps and helping victims develop skills to earn a living; and,

- write to your government officials and urge them to support the repeal of the Blasphemy Laws and to promote equal and just treatment of religious minorities in Pakistan.

7. Support organizations like OFWI that work in this area financially so that we can continue our work.

8. Finally, pray and then pray some more.

Appendix B

RELIGIOUS FREEDOM IN EGYPT AND IRAQ

A Statement by Rev. Majed El Shafie

President and Founder of One Free World International
before the Subcommittee on Africa, Global Health, and
Human Rights of the United States House of Representatives
Committee on Foreign Affairs
Christopher H. Smith (R-NJ) (Chairman)

November 17, 2011

INTRODUCTION

WE WOULD LIKE TO THANK the members of the Subcommittee on
Africa, Global Health, and Human Rights for the opportunity to
present our comments and recommendations on this important
matter of religious freedom. Our mission and calling is to stand
up for religious minorities and individuals around the world who
are being persecuted because of their personal beliefs. Our goal
in presenting these recommendations is to encourage the United
States to step up to the plate and take a principled stand for justice
and freedom for religious minorities that are voiceless, vulnerable, and oppressed.

We have been asked to comment specifically on the situation in Egypt and Iraq based on our extensive experience with religious freedom issues in these countries. Our work is not limited to these countries, however, and we would be remiss under the circumstances if we did not include some brief mention of the issues facing religious minorities in Afghanistan and Pakistan, especially given their central role in U.S. foreign policy at the present time.

Freedom of religion is a fundamental, universal right that speaks to the very core of what it means to be human. The basic freedom to believe in (or not believe in) and to practice the religion of one's choice (or equally to refrain from any religious practice) forms the very basis of human dignity and is a pre-requisite for true equality under the law. This right is recognized both by U.S. and international law as foundational and intrinsic to any truly free society, and without freedom of religion experience has shown that there can be no democracy, peace, or security.

In order to live up to its stated commitment to global religious freedom, the United States must take a more comprehensive and proactive approach to this issue, and it must take immediate steps to improve integration of freedom of religion considerations within its overall foreign policy. Although we will not dwell extensively on institutional issues, we would like to note that in order for this shift to take place, both the Office of Religious Freedom and Ambassador-at-Large must be elevated to the status envisioned by Congress in the *International Religious Freedom Act*. Such concrete steps will send a strong message that the United States is committed to religious freedom as part of its vital foreign policy interests, thereby enabling the United States to have a positive impact on the behaviour of the countries examined in these comments.

We also felt it necessary to briefly comment on some aspects of the International Religious Freedom Report's portrayal of the situation in Egypt and Iraq. Because this report inevitably shapes the perceptions of U.S. decision-makers, we are concerned that the State Department's analysis may lead some to underestimate the seriousness of the situation facing religious minorities in both countries. The need for action is urgent due to the historic circumstances facing these countries and the United States needs to take immediate and decisive action in its relations with these states.

To this end, we recommend that the United States explicitly link its aid and trade relationship with each of these countries to positive progress with regard to freedom of religion. In the case of both Egypt and Iraq, the U.S. government cannot continue to provide billions of dollars of military aid with 'no strings attached' to governments that refuse to protect (and even directly attack) their religious minorities. The United States must also make religious freedom a priority in its diplomatic and bilateral relations with both countries, and actively hold each government accountable for its failure to uphold religious freedom. As part of these efforts, the United States should seek out multilateral partnerships to enhance the effectiveness of its efforts.

Both Egypt and Iraq are entering a critical period of transition in their respective history. Both have recently emerged from decades of dictatorship, and both are, in different ways, trying to forge their own path toward a stable democracy. In both cases, the United States is in a position to help determine whether each country goes down the path of freedom and the rule of law or a path of extremism and sectarian violence. To its credit, the United States, including the present administration, has repeatedly and publicly reiterated its commitment to promote and defend freedom of religion in this region and around the world. While such strong public endorsements of religious freedom are an important first step, the time has come for the reality of U.S. foreign policy to live up to the rhetoric.

ABOUT REV. MAJED EL SHAFIE AND ONE FREE WORLD INTERNATIONAL (OFWI)

Reverend Majed El Shafie, President and Founder of One Free World International (OFWI), was born in Egypt to a prominent Muslim family of judges and lawyers. He was detained and severely tortured by Egyptian authorities after he converted to Christianity and began advocating equal rights for Egyptian Christians. Sentenced to death, he fled Egypt by way of Israel and settled in Canada in 2002, establishing OFWI to share a message of freedom, hope, and tolerance for religious differences and to promote human rights in this area through advocacy and public education.

As a young law student, Rev. El Shafie tried to work within the Egyptian system to secure equal rights for Christians by beginning a ministry and human rights organization, which in just two years grew to 24,000 members. Through numerous operations to investigate allegations of persecution against Christians, assist them in escaping persecution and other hardship, build churches, and build bridges between Muslims and Christians, Rev. El Shafie gained a great deal of knowledge and insight into the persecution of the Christian community in Egypt both by the government and by society at large.

Rev. El Shafie has been invited to speak in churches and synagogues across Canada and the United States and has been interviewed by numerous magazines, newspapers, and broadcast media, both religious and secular. He has also provided expert evidence for numerous courts and tribunals on behalf of individuals seeking protection in Canada and the United States. He has appeared three times before the Canadian Parliament's Sub-Committee on International Human Rights in Ottawa and once before the Parliamentary Coalition against Antisemitism's inquiry into antisemitism in Canada. He has built bridges with politicians inside and outside North America and addressed these issues directly with cabinet ministers and high-level officials in the Canadian government, including the Prime Minister's Office, in order to help educate decision-makers about the on-going issue of religious persecution around the world.

Never one to back down from an opportunity to stand against injustice, Rev. El Shafie has travelled to countries such as Iraq, Pakistan, and Afghanistan, where he has met face-to-face with top government officials, confronting them with evidence of human rights abuses in their countries and the failure of their governments to address these issues, also documenting some of these missions for his new feature-length documentary film, *Freedom Fighter*. OFWI has built an extensive network of trusted local sources in 28 countries around the world and where possible Rev. El Shafie visits areas of concern personally to see firsthand what the threats are. OFWI also cooperates with and relies on other trusted human rights organizations and media sources as necessary in order to ensure that it can help as many as possible.

RELIGIOUS FREEDOM

Freedom of Religion as a Human Right and in International Law

Recognition of the rights of individuals and nations, minorities and majorities, is basic. Ultimately everyone is in some respect or at some time or place a member of a minority and one need only consider one's own position but for a moment in order to see the importance of respecting the rights of others and the universal nature of this principle, known in the Christian tradition as the Golden Rule, or "Do unto others as you would have others do unto you".

Human beings have learned this painful lesson the hard way over thousands of years of violations of this foundational principle. As a result, communities and humanity as a whole have sought ways to promote respect for these lessons learned by enshrining the principle in constitutions and international documents such as the *Universal Declaration of Human Rights* (UDHR) and the *International Covenant on Civil and Political Rights* (ICCPR).

The UDHR, while not in itself binding, is considered by international law experts to reflect customary international law which in turn is binding on states. The UDHR states in Article 18 that,

> Everyone has the right to freedom of thought, conscience and religion; this right includes freedom to change his religion or belief, and freedom, either alone or in community with others and in public or private, to manifest his religion or belief in teaching, practice, worship and observance.[1]

However, it is not necessary to rely on general principles of morality or international law or even less on mere declarations of principle or aspiration in order to establish the rights of religious minorities. A large part of the world community has expressly agreed to submit to binding international law in this matter by signing or acceding to the ICCPR. Article 18 of the (ICCPR) states that,

1. Everyone shall have the right to freedom of thought, conscience and religion. This right shall include freedom to have or to adopt a religion or belief of his choice, and freedom, either individually or in community with others and in public or private, to manifest his religion or belief in worship, observance, practice and teaching.

2. No one shall be subject to coercion which would impair his freedom to have or to adopt a religion or belief of his choice.

3. Freedom to manifest one's religion or beliefs may be subject only to such limitations as are prescribed by law and are necessary to protect public safety, order, health, or morals or the fundamental rights and freedoms of others.[2]

Freedom of religion requires that all members of a given society are not only able to live without fear, but are also free to meaningfully participate in all aspects of their society without having to divorce their fundamental beliefs from their participation as citizens. Religious freedom touches the very core of human dignity and identity, and the ability to believe in and practice according to one's religion of choice is a pre-requisite for true equality under the law.

Freedom of Religion in U.S. Law and Diplomacy

In order for the United States to live up to its responsibility as the 'leader of the free world,' it is not enough that the American government respect the rights and freedoms of its citizens within U.S. borders. The United States must ensure that its foreign policy is consistent with the fundamental values that form the basis of American society and identity. There is no question that freedom of religion, as articulated in the *United States Constitution*, is one such basic and universal right that is central to both the American legal system and society at large.

The First Amendment of the *Constitution* clearly states that the U.S. government "shall make no law respecting an establishment of religion, or prohibiting the free exercise thereof."[3] Although the scope of the so-called "Establishment Clause" and the "Free Exercise Clause" has been the subject of some debate, the placement of this guarantee in the first clause of what is commonly referred to as the *Bill of Rights* clearly indicates a desire by the founders of the United States to enshrine freedom of religion as a foundational principle of the new nation. Article VI of the *Constitution* further ensures that individuals will not be excluded from participating in government on the basis of their religion, by prohibiting the "requirement" of any kind of "religious test ... as a Qualification for any Office or public Trust under the United States."[4]

The foundational role played by religious freedom in the United States is eloquently expressed in the preamble of the *International Religious Freedom Act* of 1998, where Congress stated that:

> The right to freedom of religion undergirds the very origin and existence of the United States. Many of our Nation's founders fled religious persecution abroad, cherishing in their hearts and minds the ideal of religious freedom. They established in law, as a *fundamental right* and as a *pillar of our Nation*, the right to freedom of religion. From its birth to this day, the United States has prized this legacy of religious freedom and honored this heritage by standing for religious freedom and offering refuge to those suffering religious persecution.[5] (emphasis added)

Indeed, freedom of religion is absolutely intrinsic to the broader system of rights and freedoms that underpin the United States as a society and a nation. As President Obama acknowledged in his 2009 Cairo speech, "[f]reedom in America is *indivisible* from the freedom to practice one's religion."[6] Ever since the birth of the United States, American leaders have recognized that no society can be truly free if it denies an individual's inviolable right to believe and practice his or her religion of choice.

For U.S. foreign policy to be truly 'American' it must be reflective of and consistent with core American values, including freedom of religion, especially given the centrality of this principle in shaping U.S. domestic policy and legislation. When the United States overlooks violations of religious freedom perpetrated (or condoned) by states with which it has ongoing diplomatic and economic relations, it is legitimizing the actions of those who would undermine the very principles that underlie American identity and society. Yet within the context of U.S. diplomacy and international relations, however, freedom of religion appears to be viewed as little more than a niche 'humanitarian' concern related strictly to relieving the direct human cost of persecution in individual cases. Nonetheless, while addressing and eliminating religious persecution around the world is an imperative for all nations—and it forms the core of our mission—religious freedom involves more than simply the absence of persecution or discrimination.

Religious Freedom and Egypt

1. The Mubarak Regime

Egypt is a predominately Muslim country with a population of approximately 77 million. Prior to the advent of Islam, Egypt was a primarily Christian country. Nevertheless, Christians today account for only about 10% of the population and do not enjoy the same rights as their Muslim countrymen. Recent events have caused a sea-change in the governance of the country, but the prognosis for Egypt is not nearly as positive as most international observers and optimists in policy-making positions would like to think.

Despite Egypt's attempts to portray itself as a democracy, it has been ruled for decades as a dictatorship by successive presidents, most recently Hosni Mubarak. The only religions recognized by the government have been Islam, Christianity, and Judaism. Islam is the dominant and official religion and Islamic fundamentalism is a powerful force. Anti-semitism has also been on the rise even though the Jewish community in Egypt is virtually non-existent and the few remaining members are mostly elderly individuals.

The Mubarak regime walked a fine line between opposing the extremists and appeasing them in order to maintain its hold on power. While extremists were closely monitored by the regime for anti-government activity, as long as their activities were focused on minorities the authorities paid little attention. Minorities, on the other hand, were left at the mercy of the extremists due to fears that any perceived government support could have turned the extremists against the authorities. During this period extremists also penetrated many government agencies, especially local positions, and were able to exercise influence over government action or inaction in many cases. As a result, the Egyptian government has long paid lip-service to human rights conventions and international conferences for the protection of religious freedom and human rights, but the reality has been quite different.

During a tumultuous spring of 2011, however, the world watched with incredulity as the Egyptian people forced President Mubarak to step down after more than 30 years, raising hopes that a democratic, peaceful government would take his place. The government is currently in the hands of a transitional military council as the country prepares to hold elections to determine its future direction. At the same time, the only group with any substantial support and ability to organize for those elections is the Muslim Brotherhood which, despite its rhetoric, has never renounced its extreme ideals and objectives for Egyptian society. It is the ideological parent of terrorist movements such as Hamas and Al-Qaeda and members and supporters are behind daily forced conversion attempts, violent attacks, and torture against Egyptian Christians. With a profoundly religious, largely uneducated population (illiteracy is approximately 30%) there is great reason to be concerned for the future.

2. Day-to-day Experiences

In the meantime, the bureaucracy and local government positions remain in the hands of the same people as during the Mubarak regime. As a result, little positive change can be expected in the day-to-day lives of religious minorities who experience serious violations of their rights on a daily basis, ranging from discrimination in official and civil matters such as employment, to intimidation, threats, and physical violence against property and the person, including death. Police and security forces typically do not come to the assistance of religious minorities and often charge the victims if they try to lay a complaint. When confronted by state security forces members of religious minorities face the very real possibility of torture, which international observers, including the United Nations, confirm is a systemic problem in the country.

AFP

A man holds up a blood-soaked cloth during demonstrations in Cairo on October 9, 2011.

Even though Christianity is recognized by the government, Christians are treated as second-class citizens in every respect and left at the whim and mercy of Islamic extremists. Members of unrecognized religions, such as Bahá'í's, and Muslim converts to Christianity face even greater challenges in the most basic transactions, from obtaining an education or owning property, to marriage and divorce or burying their dead, because of their inability to obtain official recognition of their religious status on identity documents. Converting to Islam is easy, but Muslims who convert to other religions find it virtually impossible to make the change official, not to mention being faced with the threat of death for apostasy from Islamic extremists and family members. Moreover, a child whose parent converts to Islam is automatically registered as a Muslim, regardless of the child's or the other parent's wishes, thus exposing the child to the apostasy threat if they choose to identify with Christianity or another minority.

Despite the restrictions, life has been tolerable for most Egyptian Christians but only as long as they maintain a low profile and bear their circumstances in silence. They must constantly be on their guard against any real or perceived offence to their Muslim neighbours which can result in everything from simple harassment and property damage to the torture and death of the perceived offender(s) or their family members. Christian girls face kidnapping and forced marriage to Muslim men and related forced conversion. While government agencies are sometimes directly involved either officially or unofficially, the perpetrators most often are family members, neighbours, friends, employers, or local mobs, often with the tacit approval or encouragement of the police or other government agencies.

The offence that can bring on the wrath of the Muslim community, leaving the Christian with no option but to flee for their safety or their life, can be anything as simple as a personal or business dispute, dating a Muslim, explaining Christianity to a Muslim or helping a Muslim convert to Christianity, coming to the aid of a Christian who had been forced to convert to Islam, or refusing themselves to convert. Often the purported offence is based on simple allegations, inferences, or a misinterpretation of the facts.

In a society that is not closed and private like North American society, once a Christian has attracted the attention of Muslim extremists, even inadvertently or through the innocent exercise of their right to freedom of religion, they are marked in society and cannot escape the threats and persecution. Moreover, if the government security services have been involved in the incident, the unfortunate Christian will likely have been placed on an internal watch-list.

3. Hope for the Future?

The revolution that began on January 25, 2011 raised the hopes of Egyptians and the international community alike for a new era of freedom and democracy. The future, however, begins today and the signs are not good. Whether the Muslim Brotherhood and other Islamic extremists will move into control of the government is almost a foregone conclusion. In any event, their influence has been growing in the absence of any force determined to keep them in check and regardless of the shape the new government will take, Muslim extremists will unquestionably have a strong influence in the coming regime.

The signs for minorities in the current situation are foreboding. Weeks before the revolution, one of the most destructive attacks on a Christian church in many years killed at least 21 and injured more than 70 at an Alexandria church during a New Year's mass. After the revolution, on the other hand, there have been eleven major attacks against Christians that have been significant enough to attract the attention of the media. Many of these have been perpetrated by Muslim mobs such as one on September 30, 2011 in

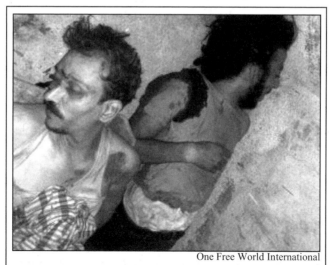

One Free World International
Victims of the October 9, 2011 massacre in Cairo.

which a church and several Coptic homes and businesses were burned down. On October 9, 2011, however, the world watched in horror as the army turned in full force with a vicious attack against peaceful Coptic demonstrators who were demanding only that the interim government provide protection against an ever-escalating series of attacks. Twenty-seven were confirmed dead (although our sources indicate that the number is likely much higher) as the army fired indiscriminately into the crowd of Christian protesters with live ammunition and drove armoured vehicles and tanks into the crowd, ruthlessly crushing any demonstrators in their path.

Religious Freedom and Iraq

The area comprising modern-day Iraq has been populated since ancient times by numerous successive civilizations. As in much of the Middle East, Christianity was once the dominant religion and its presence pre-dates the existence of Islam by several centuries and earlier various indigenous beliefs prevailed. Beginning in the 7th century, however, Islam spread through the region, mostly violently, leaving Christians and other local religions a frightened minority, subdued and subject to the Islamic majority.

Under Saddam Hussein's secular Ba'athist party, however, Iraqi minorities shared a relatively equal existence with their Muslim compatriots and, despite the regime's other failures, experienced a measure of prosperity in business, education, and society. With the invasion and subsequent insurgency, however, the fragile balance collapsed as the majority Sunni and Shi'a Muslims, encouraged by religious extremists from within and without, began vying for influence.

A once rich and diverse population is rapidly becoming more and more homogenous. Prior to the 2003 intervention by the United States-led coalition, Christians numbered an estimated 800,000 to 1 million, possibly as high as 1.4 million, but not more than approximately 3% of the population. It is estimated that eight years later only some 400,000-500,000 remain. Yezidis, with 4,000 year-old roots in the area, are estimated at 500,000 compared to 700,000 only a few years ago. Sabean Mandaeans are another minority unique to the region. With only some 60,000-70,000 worldwide, of whom approximately 50,000 resided in Iraq before the invasion, the Iraqi population is now an estimated 5,000-6,000. As members have fled Iraq, this close-knit community whose very continuation depends on its ability to maintain close community ties, faces being scattered around the globe and lost forever. The Jewish community was once a thriving minority whose presence in Iraq dates from some 2,600 years ago but it has been reduced to a handful of individuals who live in anonymity, and Bahá'í's number about 2,000 members who are scattered across the country.

Sunni and Shi'a Muslims and Kurdish separatists in the north all have large, heavily-armed militias and access to outside support, often from foreign extremist groups. Iraqi Christians and other minorities, however, are tiny communities which refuse to arm themselves or to compromise their non-violent beliefs in order to protect themselves. Christians in particular are further prevented from seeking outside help for fear of giving credence to accusations of suspect loyalties, despite the 2,000-year tradition of Christianity in the area, and thus imperilling their situation even further. Despite, or perhaps because of, their non-violent principles, Iraqi minorities are caught in the crossfire as Sunni and Shi'a factions continue to attack each other and both, in turn, attack the Christians and other minorities.

An estimated 4 million Iraqis have been displaced by the violence, 2 million internally and another 2 million as refugees, mostly in Syria, Jordan, and other surrounding countries. Of these, a vastly disproportionate number are Christians, or about a quarter of all Iraqi refugees compared with 3% of the population. Most minorities cannot stay in these countries where they cannot find work and where they continue to face discrimination as foreigners but, unlike Muslim Iraqis, also because they are, once again, of a different religion than the local Muslim population. On the other hand, they cannot return to Iraq where their jobs, homes, lives, and communities have been destroyed and where they would face further threats, torture, and possibly even death.

Although the Iraqi government has had some success in stabilizing the security situation, it has not succeeded in decisively stemming the insurgency or creating the conditions that would allow Iraqis to move on and create a prosperous society and as Western forces prepare to leave Iraqi authorities fully responsible

One Free World International

One Free World International

Rev. Majed El Shafie visits Our Lady of Salvation Church in Baghdad which was attacked in October 2010 with over 50 dead.

there is reason for concern. The Iraqi constitution provides some limited recognition of religious rights but it has serious flaws, from fundamental ambiguities that leave the door open to interpretations mandating the implementation of shariah law to conflicting provisions regarding the respective supremacy of Islamic principles or the rights enumerated in the constitution.

Many provisions require implementing legislation and others will not be clarified until the courts weigh in or a constitutional reform process takes place.

Yet despite the *prima facie* religious rights afforded in theory by the Iraqi Constitution, there is an undeniable and unacceptable gap between its promises and the reality faced by minorities in their day-to-day lives. Not only are there fundamental flaws in the text itself, but there is also a systemic lack of enforcement of the protections articulated in the constitution. The resulting culture of impunity has enabled extremist groups and left religious minorities in danger of being wiped out by what can only be described as a concerted and widespread campaign aimed at eliminating Christians and other non-Islamic minorities from Iraq.

Extremists have employed a variety of violent tactics. In certain areas, Christians and other minorities have been forced to pay *jizya*, an Islamic tax on non-Muslims akin to protection money. Under threat to convert to Islam, they must pay the *jizya*, leave, or be killed. Churches and priests have been targeted with the aim of terrorizing parishioners. Basic extortion, kidnappings, and murders are typically informed as much by religious considerations as they are by criminal aims. While the Constitution commits the state to protecting the religious sites of all religions, Sunni and Shi'a militias continue to intermittently attack each other's places of worship and Christian churches.

In this regard, over 50 people were killed in a bloody assault and siege on Our Lady of Salvation Church in Baghdad on October 31, 2010. On August 15, 2011 a church in Kirkuk was bombed in the midst of a wave of deadly attacks on a variety of targets across Iraq in which over 70 were killed. While fortunately no one at the church was hurt as a priest narrowly escaped injury, the physical damage was significant. However, this attack came less than two weeks after an August 2, 2011 car-bomb attack on another church in Kirkuk injured 13 neighbourhood residents and car-bombs near two other Kirkuk churches were discovered and dismantled with only minor damage to one of the churches.

While the majority of the outright attacks against Christians and other minorities are not directly perpetrated by government agencies—although in some cases government-allied militias or even individual government officials have been implicated—there is a

One Free World International

Rev. Majed El Shafie with Iraqi Vice-President Tareq al-Hashemi.

systemic lack of enforcement of protective laws. In the case of Attra Qiryaqous, for example, a young man who was shot and left for dead after a demanded ransom was not paid in 2007, not a single person has been arrested or charged and brought to justice. This could be taken as an isolated case, but unfortunately it is not. Moreover, a police guard who came across Attra in the hospital would not have hesitated to "finish the job" if he had not been held off by by-standers and some of the gang-members responsible for kidnapping and torturing him wore police uniforms.

Clearly no government can be expected to solve every crime that occurs within its borders; however, the government's efforts in this regard set the tone and an example for the population. Unfortunately, the Iraqi authorities have time and again failed in the area of enforcement. Moreover, what little action has been taken has come in response to events that have brought international scrutiny, such as the October 2010 church attack, where the authorities had no choice but to respond. Such selective action is an abdication of responsibility on the part of the authorities and sends the wrong message to criminals and religious extremists as well as average Iraqis. To the minorities, on the other hand, it sends the message that the government is not committed to protecting their rights.

Religious Freedom: Pakistan and Afghanistan

Pakistan is a key ally in the United States' effort to ensure the stability of the region and especially because of its nuclear capability. Yet the country's commitment to American interests in the region is suspect at best, as confirmed with the discovery in 2011 of Osama Bin Laden's hiding-place. Its commitment to human rights and religious freedom is certainly at least equally questionable. The issues are far too complex and broad-ranging to address in this brief statement; however, we would like to take this opportunity to briefly mention two issues, namely the brick factories where poor Pakistani Christians and other minority members are forced to work in indentured servitude in a form of modern-day slave camp where they live and work with their families in appalling conditions and the Pakistani blasphemy laws.

Minority rights groups and others have long advocated the repeal of Pakistan's vague and draconian blasphemy laws, sections 295B and 295C of the penal code, which mandate life imprisonment for defiling, damaging, or desecrating a copy of the Koran or an extract from it and life imprisonment or death for derogatory remarks, direct or indirect, against the Islamic prophet Mohammed. Section 295C reads:

> 295-C. Use of derogatory remarks, etc., in respect of the Holy Prophet: Whoever by words, either spoken or written, or by visible representation or by any imputation, innuendo, or insinuation, directly or indirectly, defiles the sacred name of the Holy Prophet Muhammad (peace be upon him) shall be punished with death, or imprisonment for life, and shall also be liable to fine.[7]

The blasphemy laws are typically used to terrorize minorities and pursue personal scores and vendettas but once accused, even if acquitted, the hapless victim is not safe from murder by frenzied mobs. On March 2, 2011, two months after the government's weak response to the January 4, 2011 assassination of Salman Taseer, Governor of Punjab, who was killed by his own security guard for his opposition to the blasphemy laws, Shabhaz Bhatti, the country's first Christian Minister for Minority Affairs, was killed for the same reason.

Afghanistan, on the other hand, is 99% Muslim and religious freedom is for all intents and purposes non-existent in a country that claims all its citizens are Muslim. It has tiny historic communities of Hindus, Sikhs, and others, but all indigenous Christians (whose numbers are impossible to determine but have been estimated by the State Department at 500-8,000) are converts from Islam and must not only worship secretly but must even keep their very conversion secret due to the threat of death for apostasy. The immediate threat is from family, neighbours, or co-workers but converts have no relief even from the Western-backed government. In the summer of 2010, a television program focused on exposing converts led to a public outcry and a campaign that was pushed by a leading parliamentarian and supported by President Karzai himself, to find and execute converts. Several converts were arrested and Western aid organizations suspended while numerous converts fled the country.

RELIGIOUS FREEDOM IN U.S. FOREIGN POLICY

In the *International Religious Freedom Act,* the United States has established a unique mechanism with enormous potential to foster positive change around the world with regard to freedom of religion. We would like to commend the United States government for taking such an important (and virtually unparalleled) step toward making religious freedom a true focus of its foreign policy. We have consistently and actively supported recent efforts by the Canadian government to introduce similar structures into Canada's foreign policy framework, and we sincerely hope that our government will adopt the lessons from the American experience.

Unfortunately, half-hearted implementation by the Clinton, Bush, and now the Obama administrations, along with a systemic subordination of religious freedom to other foreign policy objectives, has hindered the realization of the promise of *IRFA* and threatens to undermine the effectiveness and legitimacy of U.S. policy on global freedom of religion specifically, and its foreign policy in highly religious regions more broadly (as outlined in part V below).

The prevailing view with the American foreign policy establishment of religious freedom as distinct from the more 'traditional' focuses of diplomacy and international relations—such as peace, security, and, more recently, fostering democracy—has led to a perpetual subordination of freedom of religion to other, more 'vital' concerns. However, experience has shown us that this approach is not only morally untenable, but also fundamentally flawed. In a world where religion holds an enduring (and arguably increasing) relevance, the absence of religious freedom has far-reaching implications beyond individual abuses that must be taken into account in the formulation of foreign policy as even a cursory review of history shows that societies that restrict religious freedom are far more likely to experience profound social upheaval that jeopardizes the long-term survival of democracy in the state in question.

At the same time, freedom of religion must not be viewed as merely a 'means to an end,' as this will lead to a similar result, namely compromising the 'means' (religious freedom) for the sake of the 'ends' (such as national security). Any diplomatic initiatives on behalf of religious freedom must be premised on a commitment to its intrinsic value as an inalienable right vested in individuals on the basis of their humanity alone. However, the realization that a denial of this fundamental right impacts all other U.S. interests will help to give it the priority it deserves.

Need for a Comprehensive and Proactive Approach to Religious Freedom

Despite the goal of *IRFA* to prioritize freedom of religion, this issue remains marginalized within U.S. foreign policy. While case-specific interventions are essential and, in a very real sense, can be credited with saving numerous lives, religious freedom must be more than a 'niche' concern focused primarily on *ad hoc* interventions. In this regard, the United States has acknowledged the role of religious freedom as a fundamental pre-requisite not only for the existence of stable, rights-based democracies, but also for international peace and security. In her remarks at the release of the latest International Religious Freedom Report, Secretary of State Hillary Clinton stated that

> ...it is [the United States'] core conviction that religious tolerance is one of the *essential elements not only of a sustainable democracy but of a peaceful* society that respects the rights and dignity of each individual. People who have a voice in how they are governed—no matter what their identity or ethnicity or religion—are more likely to have a stake in both their government's and their society's success. *That is good for stability, for American national security, and for global security.*[8] (emphasis added)

This conviction, however, has not been translated into practice, as the State Department has taken a very narrow view of the role of religious freedom in U.S. foreign policy. Its freedom of religion initiatives have been primarily *reactive*, consisting almost entirely of *ad hoc* measures triggered by specific instances of persecution— and even these have been applied very selectively subject to other 'overriding' political considerations.

While we steadfastly endorse the notion that violations of religious freedom must be met with consequences (as discussed in part V below), the United States must also implement a *pro-active* long-term policy aimed at promoting religious freedom as a key component of its overall foreign policy. The United States must not only respond decisively when religious freedom is denied, it must also work consistently and positively to promote the ability of all individuals in all places to be full participants in their societies irrespective of their religious beliefs or practice. Interventions in individual instances of persecution must be part of an overall, concerted strategy to actively promote the creation of free and inclusive societies where such instances of persecution will not occur in the first place.

Prioritizing and Integrating Religious Freedom in Overall U.S. Foreign Policy

Not only does the United States need to adopt a more comprehensive and proactive approach to the issue of global religious freedom, it also needs to take immediate steps to ensure that this issue is both prioritized in and effectively integrated into its broader foreign policy apparatus. While it is not our purpose to engage in a detailed examination of the structural and institutional dynamics around freedom of religion in U.S. foreign policy, it must be emphasized that the current institutional commitment to religious freedom falls short of the broad-based emphasis on freedom of religion envisioned by Congress in *IRFA*. Section 2 of *IRFA* clearly states that

(b) It shall be the policy of the United States …:

…(3) To be vigorous and flexible, reflecting both the *unwavering commitment* of the United States to religious freedom and the desire of the United States for the most effective and principled response, in light of the range of violations of religious freedom by a variety of persecuting regimes, and the status of the relations of the United States with different nations.

…(5) Standing for liberty and standing with the persecuted, to use and implement appropriate tools in the United States foreign policy apparatus, including diplomatic, political, commercial, charitable, educational, and cultural channels, to promote respect for religious freedom by all governments and peoples.[9] (emphasis added)

Even a cursory examination of the current U.S. foreign policy mechanism reveals both a lack of "unwavering commitment" to religious freedom and a failure to integrate freedom of religion considerations into the full range of foreign policy initiatives envisaged in *IRFA*.

The type of institutional integration and prioritization outlined briefly below will foster a balanced and multi-faceted approach that will be responsive both to global realities and individual contexts. Moreover, it will communicate to the entire U.S. foreign policy establishment that religious freedom is a key objective that forms a vital part of U.S. interests. Finally, and most importantly, these reforms will send a clear message to the governments discussed in this report that the United States is committed to religious freedom as a key component of its foreign policy interests, which will enhance its ability to both effectively address the systemic violations of religious freedom outlined earlier in this statement and promote meaningful change in these countries in accordance with the recommendations herein.

1. The Role of the Office of Religious Freedom and Ambassador-at-Large

The subordination of the Ambassador-at-Large for Religious Freedom, and the marginalization of the Office of Religious Freedom more generally, within the State Department must be addressed. According to *IRFA,* the Ambassador-at-Large is to be the *"principal adviser* to the President and the Secretary of State regarding matters affecting religious freedom abroad".[10] Yet one of the most common criticisms of the Office is that, contrary to normal State Department procedure and the evident intention of Congress, the Ambassador-at-Large reports not to the Secretary of State directly, but to the Assistant Secretary of State for Democracy, Human Rights, and Labor. In order for religious freedom to receive the priority it deserves in U.S. foreign policy, the Ambassador-at-Large must be in a position to be consulted directly by the Secretary of State and other key decision-makers when formulating broader policy and making key decisions.

Moreover, the Office of Religious Freedom must be given appropriate priority in the overall scheme of United States policy. The recent two year delay in filling the position of Ambassador-at-Large sends the message to both U.S. foreign policy officials and to the world at large that freedom of religion is little more than an afterthought.[11] It is vital that the Office and the Ambassador be given sufficient attention and resources not only to carry out their advisory and reporting duties, but also to effectively incorporate religious freedom expertise into the broader State Department context.

2. Effectively Integrating Religious Freedom into Broader U.S. Foreign Policy

Religious freedom must be effectively integrated and prioritized not only within the State Department apparatus, but also into the foreign policy initiatives undertaken by other agencies and departments—such as USAID, the Department of Defense, the Department of Homeland Security, the Office of the U.S. Trade Representative, and others. Once again, the practice of the United States must reflect the recognition that freedom of religion is not merely a peripheral 'humanitarian' concern, but it affects every single aspect of U.S. foreign policy—including security and counter-terrorism policy. One of the concrete steps needed is to follow through with the creation of the position of Special Adviser on International Religious Freedom on the National Security Council as proposed by *IRFA* (amending the *National Security Act of 1947*).[12] This would ensure that the impact on religious minorities of high-level security decisions in foreign theatres is taken into account by the Executive—and ensure that U.S. foreign policy reality lives up to its rhetoric on the relevance of religious freedom to issues such as global security.

3. Addressing Systemic Subordination of Religious Freedom to Other Objectives

While verbal condemnations of countries that violate religious freedom are a necessary and extremely valuable first step, 'naming and shaming' must be backed up by a demonstrable commitment to take substantive policy action against persistent offenders who fail to respond to other measures. The "Country of Particular Concern" (CPC) designation set out in *IRFA*, provides the United States government with a mandate for effective action against a country that "has engaged in or tolerated particularly severe violations of religious freedom."[13] Unfortunately other considerations—such as trade—have taken priority both in the designation of CPCs and in the determination of policy responses. Serious concerns have been raised, for instance, about the practice of 'double-hatting' (or simply citing) already existing sanctions as a 'response' to violations of religious freedom which not only conveys a lack of commitment by the United States to defending religious freedom around the world—thereby rendering its official condemnations empty and meaningless—it is also entirely ineffective in influencing the behaviour of the states in question. As a leader in global affairs and a country that has tremendous influence around the world, the United States has a responsibility translate its "unwavering commitment" to religious freedom into real and meaningful action.

RECOMMENDATIONS FOR U.S. FOREIGN POLICY IN EGYPT, IRAQ, AFGHANISTAN, AND PAKISTAN

The restrictions on religious freedom and persecution of religious minorities described earlier in this statement and U.S. integrity demand immediate and substantive action on the part of the United States. Despite the fact that President Obama stood in Cairo in June 2009 and affirmed that, "[f]reedom of religion is central to the ability of peoples to live together,"[14] religious freedom has been marginalized and subordinated to other considerations in the formulation and implementation of U.S. foreign policy toward Egypt and the other countries discussed in this statement. This trend cannot be allowed to continue. Any U.S. foreign policy efforts aimed at promoting democracy, social stability, peace, and security without taking into account the issue of religious freedom effectively ignore one of the fundamental sources of the very problem they are seeking to address and is slated to fail.

Unless meaningful steps are taken to prioritize religious freedom in U.S. relations with Egypt, Iraq, Pakistan, and Afghanistan, U.S. foreign policy in these highly religious states will not only be highly ineffective, but will also risk exacerbating tensions and insecurity in the region. We have seen firsthand how, in these societies where the role of religion as a foundational source of individual identity is particularly heightened and the acknowledged organizing principle of society itself, the absence of religious freedom forces individuals to choose between living as second class citizens, being denied the right to participate in the full benefits of society, or denying their most deeply held beliefs in order to participate in the public sphere. This is an untenable choice, and history and experience clearly demonstrate that societies where religious freedom is denied are incapable of sustaining meaningful democratic institutions and are highly susceptible to both internal and external conflict.

Moreover, ignoring the fundamental role played by religion in these states in the name of 'secularizing' U.S. foreign policy and exporting the 'separation between church and state' will lead (and already has led) to the perception of U.S. policy as threatening the religious identity of the majority community and of the state as a whole. U.S. analysis and policy measures in these highly religious societies must be based on a recognition of the historical and social role played by religion in each country and a realization that religion will continue to play a major role in the public life of each community. Therefore, U.S. policy must accept and work within this historical and social framework, and steadfastly promote the creation of free and inclusive societies while respecting the unique identity of each individual country.

The Role of the International Religious Freedom Report

We welcome the publication of the International Religious Freedom Report ("the Report"), a unique and vital instrument in the promotion of global religious freedom. Given the importance of the Report both in informing the formulation of foreign policy and, in the case of the Countries of Particular Concern (CPC), in triggering substantive policy, it is vital that the Report present not only a comprehensive record of the violations occurring in a particular state but also an analysis that accurately reflects the overall state of religious freedom in each country. While a detailed analysis of the Report goes beyond the scope of these comments, we have several key concerns regarding both the failure to designate the countries discussed in part III as CPCs and the overall approach to the dynamics of religious persecution in these countries. Far from being merely academic critiques regarding analytical method, we believe that the problems contribute to a misleading portrayal of the religious dynamics in Egypt and Iraq, in particular, which could, in turn, lead to misguided policy in the region.

1. Failure to Identify CPCs on a Coherent Basis

A source of great concern is the failure by the State Department to designate any of the four countries discussed in this statement as "Countries of Particular Concern." According to *IRFA*, a "country of particular concern" is one that "has engaged in or *tolerated* particularly severe violations of religious freedom."[15] In light of the patterns of impunity and violations outlined in part III, it is difficult to conceive of any reason why each of these countries would not meet this threshold. It is notable that, with the exception of Afghanistan, the U.S. Commission on International Religious Freedom recommended that all of the states in question receive the CPC designation in its 2011 report.[16] In light of recent events, particularly in Egypt, this recommendation has even greater force and urgency. In order for the CPC mechanism to live up to its potential, political and diplomatic considerations cannot be allowed to guide what should be an objective analysis of the condition of religious freedom in a state.

2. Concerns re Overall Approach to Country Reports

While a detailed examination of the treatment of individual incidents is beyond the scope of this statement, we have identified a number of broader issues surrounding the portrayal of the dynamics of religious persecution in these four countries that bear highlighting. Specifically, we have found that, while the Report presents an extensive catalogue of individual restrictions or violations of religious freedom, the fragmented reporting style actually obscures the overall trends and dynamics in each country.

This is partly due to the failure of the Report to draw a distinction between different classes of events, notably the important difference between attacks perpetrated by an armed majority religious group against an unarmed minority, on the one hand, and 'sectarian' violence between two armed religious factions, on the other. This is particularly problematic in the case of Iraq, where the report systematically conflates the violence perpetrated between various armed Islamic factions and the attacks by those armed factions against unarmed minorities. The Report's treatment of the religious dynamics in Egypt is similarly problematic, as the 'tit for tat' approach taken to the so-called 'sectarian violence' between the Muslim majority and the Coptic minority glosses over the fact that the latter is a vulnerable minority. This is not to suggest that violence by vulnerable minorities should be overlooked or go unreported. However, to simply include very distinct phenomena (each calling for distinct solutions) under the heading of 'sectarian violence' is profoundly misleading as to the true dynamics. While it is important to be fair by reporting all violations, the Report appears to go too far in the direction of 'balancing the score sheet'. The resulting flawed analysis leads to flawed policy.

On the other hand, the Report tends to set up a rather unhelpful (and once again misleading) rigid dichotomy between "societal actions" that restrict religious freedom, on the one hand, and official abuses by government officials, on the other. While this is undoubtedly a valid analytical distinction, its use as the basis for analysis obscures the fundamental role played by government *inaction* in enabling "societal actions". If the authorities fail to make reasonable efforts to meet their responsibilities, they encourage lawless individuals to oppress the vulnerable and in doing so, are just as guilty as the criminals and extremists who pull the trigger or set the detonator. In Iraq, for example, despite the absence of an official government policy to persecute religious minorities, the impunity with which non-state actors are allowed to attack vulnerable religious groups has enabled the rise of extremism and rendered the government effectively complicit in the violence.

Finally, there is little discussion of any follow-up or substantive action taken by the U.S. government in response to the violations summarized in the report or of any response by the government concerned. Repeated references are made to instances where U.S. officials "raised concerns" with their Egyptian and Iraqi counterparts over issues surrounding religious freedom. However, "raising concerns" should not be equated with addressing the problem. It is an invaluable first step but cannot be the sum total of U.S. actions in response to these violations.

General Recommendations

In light of the deplorable state of religious freedom in Egypt, Iraq, Pakistan, and Afghanistan, the United States must use all foreign policy tools at its disposal both to address the violations described in this statement and the State Department's Report and to ensure that the governments in question take the necessary steps to ensure long-term protection of the rights of religious minorities. As history has shown, diplomatic engagement and political dialogue—however sustained and constructive—is often insufficient.

In order for U.S. diplomatic engagement to be effective in these four countries, it must be backed by a demonstrable commitment to take substantive policy measures. If any of these governments is not willing to respond positively to the United States' representations, it must not continue its relationship with that country on a "business-as-usual" basis but be willing to disengage and make the resumption of normal relations conditional on measurable progress in the area of religious freedom. While some specific recommendations for Egypt and Iraq will be discussed in more detail in the following sections, the current section will outline some more general recommendations that apply to all four countries.

The purpose behind the recommended actions is not simply to punish violating states and voice the United States' outrage at the behaviour in question. The ultimate purpose is to see these four states take positive steps toward the protection of religious freedom by providing them with a real incentive to change their behaviour. In Pakistan, for instance, the United States must apply substantive policy measures to exert pressure on the government to repeal its blasphemy laws, while in Afghanistan such targeted measures must be used to compel the Western-backed government to desist from its officially-sanctioned policy of pursuing converts from Islam. These examples are certainly not an exhaustive list of the issues that must be addressed, or even of the ultimate goals of achieving real religious freedom, but they demonstrate areas in which the United States must begin to move beyond mere rhetoric and take real, substantive action.

1. Linking U.S. Aid to Religious Freedom

Perhaps the most effective way for the United States to encourage these states to address the state of religious freedom is to create an explicit link between that country's respect for freedom of religion and its eligibility to receive U.S. aid. Given the magnitude of U.S. contributions to each of these countries, international aid is perhaps the United States' most powerful means of exerting pressure on states that refuse to respond positively to its diplomatic efforts in matters relating to religious freedom. Moreover, the resumption of aid payments (or the return to previous levels) must be made conditional on the attainment of achievable yet substantial targets in terms of protecting freedom of religion. This approach will provide an incentive for violating states to take measurable steps while, at the same time, demonstrating the United States' unwavering commitment to religious freedom as a vital component of its foreign policy.

The legislative authority for such an explicit link between aid and religious freedom already exists within *IRFA* and the *Foreign Assistance Act* of 1961. Section 2(b) of *IRFA* clearly states that it "shall be the policy of the United States ... to seek to channel United States security and development assistance to governments other than those found to be engaged in gross violations of freedom of religion."[17] Moreover, section 405(a) of *IRFA*[18] empowers the President to authorize the "withdrawal, limitation, or suspension of" both "development assistance" (paragraph 9) and "security assistance" (paragraph 11) in accordance with the *Foreign Assistance Act*. Section 116(a) of the *Foreign Assistance Act* further states that "no assistance may be provided under this part to the government of any country which engages in a consistent pattern of gross violations of international human rights,"[19] including "particularly severe violations of religious freedom."[20] If the United States is serious about its commitment to religious freedom, it must take action based on this authority given to it by Congress to compel these countries to undertake positive change or face serious consequences.

2. Linking U.S. Trade to Religious Freedom

While the United States must not carry on 'business-as-usual' aid relationships with the countries discussed in this report so long as their respective governments refuse to take substantive steps to address the abuses occurring within their borders, all of these countries—but especially Iraq and Egypt—have significant trading relationships with the United States. In 2010, the United States exported nearly $4 billion of goods to Egypt and nearly $1.5 billion to Iraq, while importing nearly $8 billion of goods from Iraq—primarily consisting of oil and gas. According to figures compiled by the European Union and the International Monetary Fund, the United States is Iraq's top trading partner as of 2010, accounting for 26% of Iraqi exports and nearly 20% of total Iraqi trade.[21]

These economic relationships provide the United States with a significant avenue for influence over both the Iraqi and Egyptian governments if they fail to make the necessary changes to ensure the protection of religious minorities. If other policy options to this end fail, the United States must, as a last resort, curtail its trade relationship with these states. Any government that persistently refuses to protect the human rights of its citizens must not be able to count on a business relationship with the United States with 'no strings attached'—as this would amount to an outright abdication of the United States's stated commitment to global religious freedom.

At the same time, the Unites States government must identify specific steps relating to religious freedom that would lead to a resumption (or continuation, as the case may be) of normal economic relations. By setting achievable yet substantial targets for progress in the area of religious freedom in these countries, the United States can both promote positive and sincere engagement and ensure that the governments in question demonstrate a commitment to achieve measurable progress toward the protection of fundamental human rights for all their citizens. Such an approach will help prevent the perception of the measures as heavy-handed and overly punitive, while also providing a positive incentive for each respective government to make measurable changes to its behaviour.

3. Building multilateral partnerships

Based on our experience, we believe that a major hindrance to U.S. efforts to promote religious freedom in these countries is the strong reaction against perceived U.S. unilateralism. While bilateral engagement is vitally important—and indeed most of our recommendations relate to U.S. bilateral relations—in order to enhance the effectiveness and legitimacy of its policies, the United States must be willing to create partnerships with like-minded states and to strengthen its engagements with multilateral initiatives on these issues. The importance of such multilateral engagement was emphasized by Congress in *IRFA*, which states, in section 2:

(b) It shall be the policy of the United States ...:

...(4) To work with foreign governments that affirm and protect religious freedom, in order to develop

multilateral documents and initiatives to combat violations of religious freedom and promote the right to
religious freedom abroad.

To this end, the United States must broaden its partnerships with
regional organizations and countries such as Canada who share
the same commitment to global religious freedom. Working with
initiatives such as the Canadian government's newly-announced
Office of Religious Freedom, for example, will help create a coalition of states that can both assist and support U.S. efforts in these
countries.

Moreover, in order to ensure that it has the necessary moral
authority to promote religious freedom around the world, it is
vital that the United States strengthen its engagement with other
human rights initiatives and instruments. As has already been
noted above, religious freedom is intimately inter-connected with
all other human rights; therefore, any efforts to promote religious
freedom while overlooking other key rights will be incomplete at
best. Additionally, U.S. actions will be seen as more legitimate—
and not driven by narrow interests—if its efforts to uphold global
religious freedom are accompanied by corresponding efforts on
behalf of human rights more broadly.

4. Assisting Vulnerable Refugees

Despite all other efforts, victims of religious persecution often have
no option but to flee their homes to secure their safety. During the
course of our work on behalf of victims of persecution in Egypt
and Iraq in particular, we have observed the importance of refugee protection as a safety net where all other efforts have failed.
It is critical that the United States ensure that its refugee protection system is up to the task of providing this last-ditch solution.
This means ensuring that its decision-makers are knowledgeable
about issues around religious persecution and given the necessary resources so that legitimate cases can be determined in a
timely fashion. In particular, we have seen a number of Egyptian

cases rejected in the U.S. system leaving legitimate refugees without alternatives, especially when the U.S. rejection compromises their ability to claim in another country due to safe third country agreements.

Moreover, the United States must not only take all steps necessary to accept as many refugees from these countries as possible, but must also ensure that its refugee admission process prioritizes members of minorities whose circumstances and non-violent beliefs render them especially vulnerable. Unarmed minorities such as the Christians, Bahá'í's, and Sabean Mandaeans in Iraq, or the Coptic Christians in Egypt, some of whom are forbidden by their beliefs from carrying weapons or engaging in violence of any kind—even in self defence—are particularly vulnerable. Yet

One Free World International

Coptic Christians demonstrating in Cairo on October 9, 2011.

these groups do not have the option of seeking refuge in the surrounding countries where their religious beliefs and practices render them all but as vulnerable as in their country of origin.

U.S. Foreign Policy in Egypt

With the fall of the Mubarak regime, Egypt is in a state of transition. Given the United States' significant economic and political influence in Egypt, as will be outlined in more detail below, it is imperative that the United States take immediate steps to prioritize freedom of religion in its economic and political relations with the provisional military government and the future permanent government. With great influence comes great responsibility, and the United States cannot continue to stand by while the atrocities outlined in part III continue with the acquiescence and even direct participation by the military government's own security forces.

1. Linking Military Aid with Human Rights

The most important area in which the United States must take action to address the egregious violations of religious freedom in Egypt documented above is by linking U.S. military aid with real progress and substantive positive change on these issues. Since 1979, when the *Special International Security Assistance Act* was passed, Egypt has been the second largest recipient of overall U.S. aid, receiving approximately $2 billion in general and military assistance annually.[22] Since 2007, the United States has given approximately $1.3 billion annually in military aid to Egypt,[23] an amount that has been requested once again as part of the fiscal year 2012 budget.[24]

The United States cannot continue to provide essentially 'blank cheques' to a military and security establishment that not only refuses to live up to its basic responsibilities toward Egypt's most vulnerable citizens, but that is also responsible for *directly* attacking and murdering members of the Christian minority. Secretary of State Clinton is on the record as stating that the United States "believe[s] in aid to [the Egyptian] military without any conditions" and "no conditionality."[25] Yet such unconditional support for the perpetrators of the very abuses the United States government purports to condemn—and even claims to take action against—is indefensible, especially as the latest instalment of U.S. military aid will be directed to the very same military forces that, during the incidents on October 9 described above, viciously turned their guns and armoured vehicles on the crowd.

As was the case with general aid, Congress has clearly indicated its intention that U.S. military aid should not be directed at systemic violators of human rights. Section 502B(2) of the *Foreign Assistance Act* clearly states that, except under "extraordinary circumstances" warranting military assistance, "no security assistance may be provided to any country the government of which engages in a consistent pattern of gross violations of internationally recognized human rights,"[26] including severe violations of religious freedom. Once again, section 405(a) of *IRFA* empowers the President to authorize the "withdrawal, limitation, or suspension of…security assistance" (paragraph 11) to countries engaged in such violations.[27] The State Department itself attests to the violations of religious freedom taking place in Egypt, and it is time for the United States to stop subordinating religious freedom to self-interested political considerations and follow through on its moral (and legal) responsibilities. The United States cannot go on providing unconditional assistance to a military regime that has shown blatant disregard for the basic human rights of vulnerable religious minorities.

2. U.S. Diplomatic Relations with Egypt

The United States must actively prioritize religious freedom in its diplomatic relations with the Egyptian government, all the more so in this time of uncertainty and transition. Low-key diplomatic efforts are important but public statements by the United States carry enormous weight. However, the United States has, to date, failed in its responsibility to use this influence to vigorously defend the vulnerable minorities in Egypt.

This is particularly evident in the administration's muted response to the October 9 massacre. On October 10, White House Press Secretary Jay Carney issued a statement noting that "the President is deeply concerned about the violence in Egypt that has led to a tragic loss of life among demonstrators and security forces."[28] Not only is an expression of "deep concern" falling short of outright condemnation unacceptable given the horrific events that trans-pired, but equating the "loss of life" among demonstrators with that incurred by heavily armed security forces is a blatant failure to indict those actually responsible for the vicious attacks against unarmed civilians. Furthermore, a statement vigorously con-demning the attacks should have come from President Obama directly, rather than his press secretary, in order to appropriately reflect the gravity of the attacks for which responsibility must be taken by the provisional military council.

Moreover, in a call with Egyptian Foreign Minister Mohamed Kamel Amr on October 11, Secretary of State Clinton expressed U.S. support for the transitional military government's decision to "launch a transparent and credible investigation into the violence and stressed the importance of ... holding accountable all respon-sible parties with full due process of law."[29] While such support for an immediate investigation into the killings is commendable, we are unaware of any clear and substantive statements by the United States with regard to the subsequent decision by the rul-ing military council to take over the inquiry from the civilian prosecutor and 'investigate' its own actions. An 'investigation' conducted by officials falling within the chain of command of the very same forces that carried out these brutal attacks is neither "transparent" nor "credible"—and yet the United States has been silent on this development.

The United States cannot stand quietly by while the transitional government oppresses the rights of its religious minorities and engages in what can only be described as a thinly-veiled cover-up of its actions. The United States has a unique opportunity to help shape the future of the nascent Egyptian democracy, and it must take this responsibility seriously. Overlooking or downplaying such blatant violations sends the message to the Egyptian mili-tary council and the people at large that the United States is not committed to religious freedom and that it will tolerate systemic human rights abuses so long as U.S. economic interests are not directly affected.

3. Address the Rising Influence of the Muslim Brotherhood

As Egypt looks forward to future elections and the easing of restrictions on the Muslim Brotherhood, there have been indications of its rising influence in Egyptian politics, particularly through its newly established Freedom and Justice Party. The United States has been pursuing an "approach of limited contacts" with the Muslim Brotherhood,[30] and Secretary of State Clinton has stated publicly that the United States is willing to "work with all those who have a real commitment to what an Egyptian democracy should look like."[31] She has also emphasized the United States' commitment to "democratic principles," including "non-violence, respect for minority rights, and the full inclusion of women in any democracy."[32]

It is imperative that the United States translate this commitment to such key democratic principles into reality, especially in its dealings with the Muslim Brotherhood given that the Freedom and Justice Party has already shown signs of rejecting the full inclusion of minorities and women, by announcing publicly that it "rejects the candidacy of women or Copts for Egypt's presidency."[33] The United States must base its foreign policy on the realization that democracy alone is not the answer and democratic elections must not be used as either a licence to violate human rights by foreign governments or as a justification for inaction by the United States. Democracy that is not founded in and informed by universal principles of human rights and the rule of law is simply licence for mob rule and democratic institutions must be developed and protected by a government committed to enforcing and protecting human rights. In this regard, supporting the approach to democracy espoused by the Muslim Brotherhood would be a betrayal of the minorities, women, and any other vulnerable segments of the population and ultimately a betrayal of the very principles of democracy itself which can only truly exist where people have the right and unhindered ability to pursue their goals and express their individuality.

U.S. Foreign Policy in Iraq

As Iraq is on the verge of being fully responsible for its own affairs, the United States' role in Iraq is changing but its responsibility toward the Iraqi people still remains. Although the 'official' war in Iraq is drawing to a close, the troubling pattern of violations described above clearly shows that the crisis for religious minorities in Iraq is far from over. The United States must take immediate and concrete steps to help ensure that Iraq goes down the path of freedom and the rule of law rather than a path of extremism and sectarian violence which will inexorably affect both the broader security situation in the region and U.S. security interests.

1. Accountability for Enforcing the Law and Fighting Impunity

Perhaps the most important way in which the United States can have a positive impact on the state of religious freedom in Iraq is to vigorously and consistently hold the Iraqi government accountable for its systematic failure to enforce the laws protecting vulnerable groups from religious persecution. Despite the absence of an active, concerted policy on the part of the government to target and attack minorities the authorities must ultimately bear responsibility in these matters. While religious extremists have the ability even to infiltrate government positions, they must be pursued for their violations and brought to justice.

What little action has been taken by the Iraqi authorities in response to the violations outlined above has come in response to events that have brought international scrutiny, such as the October 2010 church attack—when the world was watching and there was no choice but to act. While such cases are a clear sign that the Iraqi government is failing in its responsibility toward religious minorities, they should also serve as an encouragement in that they show that Iraq is listening and sensitive to outside opinion. Consequently, they are also a call to action for the United States to step up its engagement with and scrutiny of the enforcement policies of the Iraqi government, not only to secure justice in individual cases but to help eliminate the culture of impunity within Iraq's legal system. The United States cannot sit quietly by while the Iraqi government continues to allow these crimes to go unpunished.

2. Prioritizing Religious Freedom in Bilateral Framework and U.S. Aid

In light of the imminent change in the nature of U.S.-Iraqi relations with the upcoming pull-out of U.S. troops, the United States must seize this unique (but limited) opportunity to prioritize religious freedom within its new bilateral relationship with Iraq. Of immediate concern is the fact that the Strategic Framework Agreement for a Relationship of Friendship and Cooperation between the United States of America and the Republic of Iraq,[34] which was signed in November of 2008 and still forms the legal basis of the long-term bilateral relationship,[35] makes no mention of religious freedom and only refers to human rights once as part of a vague statement about promoting Iraq's efforts in "the field of social welfare and human rights."[36] This blatant subordination of human rights in general, and religious freedom in particular, to other political considerations is not only morally unacceptable but also politically unwise. A failure by the United States to emphasize human rights during this transitional period in Iraq will only serve to perpetuate the instability and conflict in Iraq and the region as a whole with obvious broader implications.

The need to prioritize religious freedom in the United States' bilateral relations with Iraq is especially crucial in the management of U.S. aid to Iraq, particularly the $2 billion of security and military assistance that have been requested as part of the fiscal year 2012 budget.[37] While it is unnecessary to reiterate the points made above in the context of U.S. military aid to Egypt, it is valuable to state once more that the United States cannot simply sign over $2 billion to a government that has, to date, consistently failed in its responsibility to enforce the law and protect its religious minorities. While this pervasive culture of impunity can be viewed as precisely the reason why such assistance is necessary, the United States cannot simply turn over $2 billion dollars to the Iraqi government with 'no strings attached.' This security sector aid must be conditional on the Iraqi government taking clear and substantive steps toward the protection of religious freedom. The United States aid policy must be based on the realization that an Iraq that systematically ignores the violation of the basic human rights of its citizens—and allows for the rise of extremism and the influence of Iran, as discussed below—will not only fail as a democratic state but will also emerge as a grave threat to U.S. national security.

3. Act to Neutralize Influence of Iran in Iraq

While a detailed examination of Iran's role and influence in Iraq goes beyond the scope of these comments, a brief mention is necessary. The upheaval of recent years in Iraq has allowed Iran to increase its influence in the country—especially given the rise of the Shi'ite sector that has close ties to Iran. As U.S. forces prepare to withdraw at the end of the year, there is a very real risk that Iran could step into the void. This will inevitably lead to further curtailment of minority rights and a strengthening of Iran in the region. As of the preparation of this statement, 4,421 U.S. servicemen and women have given their lives for "Operation Iraqi Freedom"—and nearly 32,000 have been wounded. If the United States stands by and allows Iraq to become a satellite of Iran, the blood of all those brave American heroes will have been shed in vain.

CONCLUSION

Every member of the international community has undertaken a sacred trust to uphold fundamental human rights. There is no right more fundamental to human dignity and to truly free and inclusive societies than freedom of religion. In light of the horrific abuses of this basic right occurring throughout the world today, no country, the United States included, can say that it has fulfilled its duty to protect religious freedom and the vulnerable minorities to whom this freedom is denied. As a leader in global affairs and a country with an unmatched influence on the world stage, the United States cannot stand by while these abuses continue.

While we commend the United States for publicly stating its commitment to religious freedom—and for enshrining that commitment in law—statements of concern and condemnation must be followed up with substance and action. The full implementation of the promise of the *International Religious Freedom Act* is long overdue. Well over a decade after the creation of this first-of-its-kind legislative mechanism with incredible potential for the promotion of global religious freedom, the United States faces a moment of truth. Will it continue to treat religious freedom as an afterthought in its foreign policy and lose its moral authority as a leader on this issue, or will the United States government renew its commitment to global freedom of religion and take an unwavering stand on behalf of vulnerable minorities?

The United States is facing a choice as to how its influence will help shape the future of two would-be democracies entering a critical state of transition. This is a unique opportunity to assist both Egypt and Iraq to pursue the path of freedom and the rule of law, but inaction at this crucial juncture could have devastating consequences not only for the regions' religious minorities, but also for global stability and, therefore, the security of the United States itself. At this pivotal moment in history, will the United States choose to be part of the problem or the heart of the solution?

186

RECOMMENDATIONS: SUMMARY

The United States has the opportunity to fully implement the vision of *IRFA* and address the systemic subordination and marginalization of religious freedom in U.S foreign policy and the historic opportunity to make a long-term impact on peace, democracy, and stability in the Middle East and beyond by prioritizing freedom of religion in its dealings with Egypt and Iraq.

Religious Freedom and General U.S. Foreign Policy

1. U.S. policy must be based on the premise that religious freedom is not only a humanitarian concern, but also a *pre-requisite* for stable democracy, social stability, and global security

2. the U.S. must adopt a more comprehensive and proactive approach to religious freedom as part of its foreign policy

   • religious freedom initiatives must be fully implemented into long-term policy and not restricted to *ad hoc* interventions in individual cases

   • the U.S. must be proactive in promoting religious freedom as part of its vital foreign policy interests, and not merely reactive

3. religious freedom must be prioritized in and integrated into the mainstream of U.S. foreign policy as envisioned in *IRFA*, a process that can be facilitated by:

   • elevating the Ambassador-at-Large for Religious Freedom to the proper position in State Department hierarchy to ensure consultation on key policy decisions

- allocating sufficient resources to the Office of Religious Freedom and placing religious freedom experts in other departments

- following through with the creation of the position of Special Adviser on International Religious Freedom on the National Security Council (as proposed in *IRFA*)

- following through with substantive action against states designated as Countries of Particular Concern (CPC)

4. such concrete steps will:

- communicate to the U.S. foreign policy establishment and the world that religious freedom is a vital component of U.S. interests

- foster a balanced and multi-faceted approach to religious freedom in U.S. foreign policy

General Recommendations for U.S. Foreign Policy in Egypt, Iraq, Afghanistan, and Pakistan

1. U.S. foreign policy in these highly religious societies must be based on a recognition of the prominent role played by religion as a source of individual and collective identity

2. U.S. foreign policy officials must steadfastly promote free and fully inclusive societies while respecting the role of religion as an organizing principle of society in these countries

3. the State Department must address the unsatisfactory portrayal of the religious dynamics in these countries and designate them as Countries of Particular Concern

4. U.S. foreign aid to these countries (both general and military aid) must be explicitly linked to religious freedom and conditional on substantive progress in this area

5. the U.S. must not continue 'business-as-usual' economic relations with these states, and must be willing to curtail its trade relationships in the absence of positive progress

6. the U.S. must build multilateral partnerships with like-minded states and international bodies to enhance the effectiveness of its policies and counter perceptions of unilateralism

7. the U.S. must ensure that its refugee protection system provides an effective remedy of last resort for legitimate refugees and that members of vulnerable, unarmed minorities are prioritized

Recommendations for U.S. Foreign Policy in Egypt

1. U.S. military aid must be made conditional on substantial and measurable progress in the area of religious freedom

   • the U.S. must not continue to provide $1.3 billion annually with 'no strings attached' to a military establishment that not only fails to protect religious minorities, but also attacks them directly

2. the U.S. must make use of its influence in Egypt and prioritize religious freedom in its diplomatic relations with the transitional government

   • U.S. officials must move beyond merely "expressing concern" and hold their Egyptian counterparts accountable for their failures and direct violations of religious freedom

3. the U.S. must address the rising influence of the Muslim Brotherhood and uphold democracy not as an end to itself but as a means to promote and protect fundamental human rights

Recommendations for U.S. Foreign Policy in Iraq

1. the U.S. must actively hold the Iraqi government accountable for its failure to protect religious minorities and ensure that reforms are enacted to end systemic impunity

2. religious freedom must be prioritized in the new U.S. bilateral relationship with Iraq following the withdrawal of U.S. forces

   • religious freedom (and human rights more generally) must receive greater emphasis in existing agreements such as the *Strategic Framework Agreement*

3. U.S. aid to Iraq (especially $2 billion of security sector aid) must be conditional on significant progress toward the protection of religious freedom

4. the U.S. must act decisively to prevent Iran from stepping into the void left by the departure of U.S. forces, to ensure that American blood was not spilled in vain

Appendix C

RELIGIOUS FREEDOM IN AFGHANISTAN AND PAKISTAN

A Statement by Rev. Majed El Shafie

President and Founder of One Free World International before the Tom Lantos Human Rights Commission of the United States Congress

Frank R. Wolf (R-VA)—Co-Chairman

James P. McGovern (D-MA)—Co-Chairman

March 21, 2012

I. INTRODUCTION

Mr. Chairman and Members of the Commission, I would like to thank you for the opportunity to testify before the Tom Lantos Human Rights Commission today to present my observations and recommendations on the important subject of religious freedom in Afghanistan and Pakistan. My name is Reverend Majed El Shafie, and I am the President and Founder of One Free World International (OFWI), an international human rights organization based out of Toronto, Canada. I was born in Egypt to a prominent Muslim family of judges and lawyers. After I converted to Christianity and began advocating equal rights for

Egyptian Christians, I was detained and severely tortured by Egyptian authorities. Sentenced to death, I fled Egypt by way of Israel and eventually was resettled in Canada in 2002. Hence, my concern for religious individuals, and especially religious minorities, around the world who are being persecuted because of their personal beliefs stems from the fact that I was once one of them.

I have been asked to comment specifically on the situation in Pakistan and Afghanistan based on my experience with religious freedom issues in these countries. While my comments will focus on freedom of religion, I would be remiss if I did not highlight the deplorable human rights situation of women and children, particularly in Afghanistan, especially since this situation is intimately linked to religious freedom through its justification on the basis of restrictive, intolerant religious grounds. The need for action is urgent due to recent developments both within each country and within the region as a whole, and I would take this opportunity to call on the United States to take immediate and decisive action in its relations with these states to promote respect for religious freedom and human rights more generally.

My goal here today is to encourage the United States, as a world leader, to take a principled stand for justice and freedom for religious minorities who are voiceless, vulnerable, and oppressed. I would like to note that a comprehensive written report including my full recommendations is available upon request and will be available on the One Free World International website at www.onefreeworldinternational.org.

Freedom of conscience is a fundamental, universal right that speaks to the very heart of what it means to be human, and freedom of religion—the basic freedom to decide not only what or what not to believe in, but also to manifest that choice in one's practices—forms the very basis of human dignity and is a prerequisite for true equality under the law. As such, respect for these beliefs is a prerequisite for human dignity and true equality under the law. The right to religious freedom is recognized both by U.S. and international law as foundational and intrinsic to any truly free society, for without freedom of religion, experience has shown that there can be no lasting democracy, peace, or security. For these reasons, I would urge the United States to adopt a more comprehensive and proactive approach to this issue and take immediate steps to improve the integration of freedom of religion within its overall foreign policy particularly as it applies to Pakistan and Afghanistan.

The United States is entering a period of transition in its relations with both Pakistan and Afghanistan. In both cases, the United States is in a unique position to help determine whether each country goes down the path of freedom and respect for human rights or a path of extremism, oppression, and violence. To its credit, the United States has repeatedly and publicly reiterated its commitment to promote and defend freedom of religion in this region and around the world. While such public endorsements of religious freedom are an important first step, the time has come for the reality of U.S. foreign policy to live up to the rhetoric.

II. RELIGIOUS FREEDOM IN PAKISTAN

Background

Pakistan has been a key ally of the United States' efforts to promote stability and fight terrorism in the region, and the United States has supported the government despite serious human rights concerns. However, Pakistan's commitment to American interests in the region is suspect at best, as confirmed with the discovery in 2011 of Osama Bin Laden's hiding-place only miles from a major state military academy and installation. Its commitment to human rights in general, and religious freedom in particular, is equally questionable. Pakistan is increasingly governed by Islamic principles and influenced by Islamic extremists. As a result of the government's apparent weakness, Islamic extremists are being strengthened and support for extremist groups and parties is increasing with a direct impact on religious minorities.

About 97% of Pakistan's population adheres to either Sunni (77%) or Shi'a (20%) interpretations of Islam. The remaining 3% includes Christians, Hindus, Ahmadis, and other religions. Despite provisions ostensibly protecting religious freedom, the Pakistani Constitution, as amended in 2010, makes the "right to profess, practice, and propagate" the religion of one's choice "*subject* to law, public order, and morality"[1]—an unacceptably broad limitation that has been used to effectively undermine any ostensible guarantee of religious freedom. Laws enshrining various aspects of shari'ah reinforce the second-class citizenship of all non-Muslims and directly involve the state in persecution of minorities. Foremost among these are the so-called Blasphemy Laws (which I will discuss in more detail shortly), enacted in their current form in the early to mid-1980s. Furthermore, as recently as May 2007, Muslim parties put forward a bill called *The Apostasy Act 2006*, which proposed death for males and life imprisonment for females who change their religion from Islam. Although the bill has not been officially passed into law, the government did not oppose it, but rather sent it to a parliamentary committee for consideration. Moreover, the constitution also states that "all existing laws shall be brought in conformity with the Injunctions of Islam...and no law shall be enacted which is repugnant to such Injunctions,"[2] a provision that has been successfully used by opponents of legal reforms aimed at protecting religious freedom.

While government actors are guilty of persecution directly, many abuses of religious freedom involve local or community abuses rather than direct state action. These include attempts at forced conversion, kidnapping and rape of Christian and other minority girls, and vigilante enforcement of strict shari'ah and the Blasphemy Laws. However, the authorities are complicit by enabling these abuses through their refusal to investigate or assist victims.

My statement today focuses on the Blasphemy Laws, rape of minority girls, and slave labour camps.

Blasphemy Laws

Despite repeated promises by past regimes that they would be repealed, Pakistan's vague and draconian Blasphemy Laws remain in force and very much in use. Far from being merely a symbolic and irrelevant gesture, the blasphemy provisions are still a powerful tool in the hands of Islamic extremists—so much so that vocal opponents of these laws have paid with their lives. On March 2, 2011, Shahbaz Bhatti, Pakistan's first Christian Minister for Minority Affairs, was assassinated for his opposition to the Blasphemy Laws less than two months after Salman Taseer, Governor of Punjab, was killed by his own security guard for the same reason.

These blasphemy provisions, contained in sections 295B-C of the Pakistani Penal Code (along with sections 298 A-C that specifically target Ahmadis), mandate as follows: life imprisonment for defiling, damaging, or desecrating a copy of the Koran or an extract from it; and life imprisonment or death for derogatory remarks, direct or indirect, against the Islamic prophet Mohammed. The Blasphemy Laws are primarily used to terrorize minorities and pursue personal scores and vendettas, and their very existence undermines any effective freedom of religion in Pakistan. The definition of 'blasphemy' is so broad and vague that it constitutes an affront to any conceivable notion of the rule of law and international human rights standards. An individual can easily breach this law without intention and almost any comment or gesture can be interpreted as a violation at the accuser's whim and fancy.

The potentially unlimited scope of the 'crime' of 'blasphemy' is illustrated by section 295C, which reads:

295-C. Use of derogatory remarks, etc., in respect of the Holy Prophet: Whoever by words, either spoken or written, or by visible representation or by *any imputation, innuendo, or insinuation, directly or indirectly*, defiles the sacred name of the Holy Prophet Muhammad (peace be upon him) shall be punished with death, or imprisonment for life, and shall also be liable to fine.[3] (emphasis added)

Intimidation and threats against lawyers and judges makes defending against blasphemy charges difficult; nevertheless, the death sentence is usually overturned on appeal. However, even when the conviction or sentence is reversed, the accused has typically spent several years in prison on false charges in horrific conditions, facing daily abuse from guards and fellow inmates. Numerous accused who were acquitted by the courts have been killed by mobs or Muslim vigilantes. Others have been killed by Muslim prisoners while awaiting a verdict in their case.

Time does not allow for a comprehensive examination of the countless human rights abuses arising from the Blasphemy Laws, and the examples that follow are merely illustrative of their widespread and enduring use and how their very existence affects the daily lives of Christians even if they do not result in official charges. On February 28, 2012, Shamin Bibi, a 26-year old mother, was arrested for allegedly 'blaspheming' the Islamic prophet Mohammed, despite the fact that at least one of the alleged 'witnesses' was not even present at the time of the alleged incident. On September 28, 2011 a 13-year-old school-girl was expelled and her family forced to uproot their lives and relocate due to pressure from blasphemy accusations arising from an inadvertently misspelled word on a school assignment.

As I speak to you today, another mother (of five), Asia Noreen (better known as Asia Bibi), remains in prison under a death sentence for 'blasphemy' following a complaint by some Muslim women from her village. They had been working together in the fields when she brought them water at their request, which led to a dispute over whether they could drink the water she, a non-Muslim, had offered them. During the ensuing dispute Ms. Bibi had stated her conviction that Jesus, not Mohammed, is the true prophet resulting in an attack by an extremist mob and charges that she had insulted Mohammed. The lawyers working on her appeal have been subject to death threats, and Ms. Bibi herself has been repeatedly beaten and mistreated by Muslim prison guards.

In December 2011, Khuram Masih, a 23-year old Christian man, was charged with 'blasphemy' on false allegations of desecrating the Quran—despite a complete lack of evidence and contradictory testimony from the alleged 'witnesses'—following a dispute with his Muslim landlord over rent. In January 2012, Mr. Masih was denied bail. In June 2011, Dildar Yousef was charged with 'blasphemy' after intervening to defend his nephew from a mob of Muslim youth who were attempting to force the eight-year-old boy to recite the Islamic creed. Only 3 months earlier, Qamar David, a Christian man serving a life sentence for allegedly sending 'blasphemous' text messages, died in prison after expressing fears for his life to his legal team. The conflicting accounts of his death given by prison officials have led many to suspect that Mr. David was murdered.

Rape of Christian Girls

Pakistan acceded to the *Convention on the Elimination of All Forms of Discrimination against Women* (CEDAW) in 1996. However, despite Pakistan's outward endorsement of international standards and the symbolism of the late Benazir Bhutto's achievements as the first female prime minister of a Muslim state, the status of Pakistani women, and particularly minority women, remains of grave concern. As in many other Muslim countries, Christian and other minority girls are commonly raped by local Muslims. Cases of Christian girls who have been raped or gang-raped, either simply because they are Christians or as punishment for various actions by or disputes with the girls' family members, routinely come to our attention. With some exceptions, Pakistani police generally do not pursue these cases and even where they do, proving rape has been virtually impossible in Pakistani courts.

The so-called "Hudood Ordinances," enacted in 1979, required the rape victim to adduce four male eye-witnesses, failing which women have been charged with *zina* (adultery or fornication). The prescribed punishments are in line with strict Islamic law, up to 100 lashes or death by stoning. Amendments to these ordinances, which re-inserted the crime of rape into the criminal code, were enacted with much fanfare in 2006. However, while the reforms have addressed some of the legal problems in theory, they have been grossly inadequate and have failed to have any practical effect on the culture of impunity surrounding the rape of minority girls and the use of the threat of a charge of adultery as a means to force minority women to marry their Muslim rapists and convert to Islam.

Minority victims often do not report rape cases for a variety of reasons, including: the limitations of the relevant legislation and the ongoing adherence by local shari'ah or tribal courts (the only courts accessible for most Pakistanis) to the principles of shari'ah law which underlay the Hudood Ordinances; ignorance of their rights and the law as well as a lack of education and resources to pursue official means of redress among impoverished and often illiterate minority communities; and the social stigma associated with victims of these crimes in a conservative, religiously defined society. Official indifference or even hostility to these cases in general and/or to minority complainants in particular, along with the broader (and often violent) social pressure exerted against those who file complaints, is not only a barrier to justice in reported cases, but also a deterrent for women to file a report in the first place.

In a case that typifies the struggles faced by minority rape victims, a Christian mother of 5 was raped by two Muslim men on September 15, 2011. The police initially refused to file a complaint, and even after finally opening an investigation due to intense pressure from international advocates, police delayed a full two weeks before arresting a suspect, allowing members of the Islamic community to pressure the woman's family to drop the charges. As a result of the stress of the ordeal, the victim's elderly father died of a heart attack—and after all this it remains unclear whether the arrest will result in any meaningful punishment for the perpetrators.

The U.S. State Department's own latest report acknowledges at least two cases where victims of rape faced either official apathy or violent pressure to withdraw the charges. These include an incident on July 22, 2010, when a 12-year old Christian girl was gang raped by a group of students. Under pressure from Muslim leaders, the authorities refused to accept the complaint.[4] One day earlier, a 16-year old Christian girl was raped by three men, who subsequently abducted and tortured the victim's father after he attempted to file a claim with the authorities.[5]

Moreover, the disturbing practice of minority girls being abducted, raped, and forced to convert to Islam is not only ongoing but appears to be increasing. Although accurate statistics are difficult to compile—given the fact that most rape in Pakistan goes unreported for the reasons outlined above—recent estimates suggest that there are in excess of 700 such cases each year.[6] Women who are subjected to this horrific practice are left with few alternatives but to submit to a life of subjugation and shame at the hands of their rapists. Given the aforementioned religious laws, courts have proven unwilling to order a girl returned to her family after having sexual relations (even forced) with a man, especially if the girl becomes pregnant. If the girl successfully evades her captors, she and her family are frequently subjected to violent threats from the abductors—who are often powerful members of the Muslim community—not to mention the fact that, by returning to her non-Muslim family, the victim is now considered to be an 'apostate' under shari'ah.

On a fact-finding mission to Pakistan in 2007, I was introduced to a particularly disturbing case. My team and I met Neeha, a young Christian girl only 4 years old, who had been raped at the age of 2 ½ by the Muslim son of her father's employer. Her father, a farmer, had refused to convert when pressured to do so by his employer. In revenge, the employer's son raped the child and left her at the side of the road to die. When she was found, the hospital refused to treat her and the family was forced to seek help at a hospital in another town where news of the incident had not yet reached.

One Free World International

Neeha, a four-year-old Christian girl who was raped at age 2 ½ by the Muslim son of her father's employer.

The authorities did not bring justice to Neeha's case. The young man felt that he was entitled to inflict this unthinkable punishment on this innocent child simply because her father refused to convert to Islam and, as a Christian, had no rights. By refusing to pursue the matter, the authorities granted legitimacy to this perverted sense of entitlement. The family remained in hiding for almost four years, unable to obtain further medical help for the child. Today, Neeha and her family are safe in Canada, and earlier this month they received landed immigrant status thanks to the goodwill of the Canadian government. However, many more girls like Neeha remain voiceless and helpless at the hands of their abusers.

Labour Camps

On another fact-finding mission, I was taken undercover to view a labour camp south of Lahore. Poor Christians and members of other minorities are approached by wealthy businessmen with government connections who offer them loans. The loans are to be paid back by working at 'factories' where the workers will be provided food and shelter. In a country of extreme poverty such an offer seems an attractive option to the destitute who have no other options and no future because of their minority status. In actuality, on accepting these terms the Christians are then taken to 'factories' that function as labour camps where they are forced into what is essentially indentured servitude, or modern-day slavery.

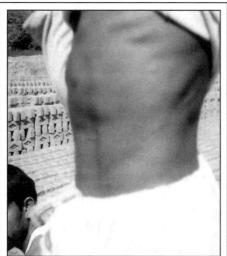

One Free World International

A Christian worker displays a lengthy scar across his abdomen from torture at a brick factory visited by Rev. El Shafie.

Our sources informed us about six such camps and provided us with the names of the 660 families at the camp my team and I visited. These families and individuals are forced to live and work under armed guard in appalling conditions, including child labour and physical abuse ranging all the way to torture. They receive minimal pay with no prospects of escape.

Accurate figures are difficult to obtain, but the latest U.S. Department of State estimates suggest that over 1.8 million people are victims of bonded labour in Pakistan[7] and the actual numbers are likely much higher. Despite the staggering scope of these abuses, the Pakistani government has taken no measures to address conditions at the camps, to prosecute those responsible under existing laws, or to provide training and education for the workers so that they can obtain proper employment.

III. RELIGIOUS FREEDOM AND THE RIGHTS OF WOMEN AND CHILDREN IN AFGHANISTAN

Background

The constitution of Afghanistan states that the country is an Islamic republic. The population is overwhelmingly Muslim, with 99% of Afghans identifying with either Sunni (80%) or Shi'a (19%) schools of Islam. The remaining 1% consists of Hindus, Sikhs, and others, including a tiny minority of secret Christians with estimates of its size varying widely from 500 to 8,000.[8] The traditional position of the authorities, however, is that all citizens are Muslim—a position that precludes any meaningful religious freedom in Afghanistan.

The government of Afghanistan is bound by its own constitution as well as by international law to respect and in fact to enforce the rights of religious minorities. Article 2 of the Afghan constitution, while recognizing Islam as the country's official religion states that,[9]

> Followers of other faiths shall be free within the bounds of law in the exercise and performance of their religious rituals.

Article 22 states that,

> Any kind of discrimination and distinction between citizens of Afghanistan shall be forbidden.

and Article 29,

> Persecution of human beings shall be forbidden. No one shall be allowed to [commit] or order torture, even for discovering the truth from another individual who is under investigation, arrest, detention or has been convicted to be punished. Punishment contrary to human dignity shall be prohibited.

To date, however, these principles have not been applied in practice, to the point where I can say with conviction that there is *no* freedom of religion in Afghanistan. Nowhere is this more evident than in the recent deliberate campaign by Afghan authorities against converts, which I will discuss in a moment, but also in on-going persecution by religious and civil authorities and their unwillingness to protect individual converts from attack by family members or other individuals in the community—all of which clearly violates Afghanistan's own constitution.

Moreover, the continued existence of civil and religious laws, in particular apostasy laws, which prevent individuals from holding, practising, or changing their religious beliefs as they choose are a grievous breach of international human rights law. A full review of religious minority issues in Afghanistan is beyond the scope of this statement, and I will, therefore, focus on two specific areas of acute urgency, namely the on-going situation related to apostasy and the treatment of converts as well as the government's current campaign against local and foreign Christians. What follows is only a sampling of the cases that have taken place in Afghanistan and even outside the country through the direction of Afghan authorities in recent years since the new constitution and the new, post-Taliban regime. Additionally, while the focus of this statement is on religious freedom, I would be remiss if I did not mention the horrific abuses endured by women and children generally, which I will also briefly highlight.

Persecution of Converts from Islam

Religious freedom is for all intents and purposes non-existent in Afghanistan given the official claim that all citizens are Muslim. Particular concern must be raised about the apostasy laws sanctioned and enforced by Islamic shari'ah courts and by Afghan authorities. These laws are implicated in countless cases of Muslims who have converted to Christianity and, as a result, have been condemned to death by shari'ah courts or civil authorities.

In many cases these judgments have been carried out while in others the converts have been forced to flee the country to save their lives.

One prominent case involved Said Musa, an Afghan convert from Islam who was arrested in May 2010, charged with 'apostasy' and sentenced to death. Although Mr. Musa was released in February 2011 following intense international diplomatic pressure, he endured sexual abuse, psychological abuse, and torture during his detention and has now obtained refuge in a third country. Another convert, Shoaib Assadullah, was arrested and threatened with execution for apostasy (leaving Islam) in October 2010 after giving a friend a copy of the New Testament. Mr. Assadullah has also been physically assaulted, threatened, and raped by fellow inmates and Afghan authorities.

While Mr. Musa's case shows that Afghan authorities are sensitive to international pressure—an outcome which should serve as an encouragement to the United States to exert its influence— these two cases are only part of a consistent pattern of similar abuses that take place on an on-going basis. The only difference in Mr. Musa's case is that his story managed to capture the attention of the international press while numerous others continue to unfold out of the limelight, as the media is focused on other issues related to the geopolitical situation in Afghanistan. In fact, both Mr. Musa's and Mr. Assadullah's cases are part of a larger, deliberate campaign to find and execute all Afghan Christians and converts initiated recently by the government of Afghanistan.

The current open campaign began in earnest when a privately run television channel aired a program on May 27 and 28, 2010 about converts to Christianity, broadcasting footage of what was purported to be Afghans being baptized and praying with western Christians. Angry protests against foreigners trying to convert Muslims took place in Kabul, prompting the government to issue official statements on the matter. Abdul Attar Khawasi, Deputy

Secretary for the lower house, stated in parliament that, "Those Afghans that appeared in this video film should be executed in public, the house should order the attorney general and the NDS [intelligence agency] to arrest these Afghans and execute them." President Hamid Karzai's spokesperson has stated that the president himself had urged his interior minister and the head of intelligence to investigate and "to take immediate and serious action to prevent this phenomenon" [the conversion of Afghans to Christianity].

The official reaction to this television broadcast was followed by a severe crackdown on the already small and beleaguered Christian community in Afghanistan. Police engaged in arbitrary and repeated searches of homes and businesses, and our sources state that at least 26 individuals believed to be converts were arrested, as well as Muslim family members of suspected converts. Some of those in custody were raped and tortured in an effort to obtain information about other converts and gatherings. As indicated above, the government has stated its intention that any individuals found to have converted will be executed and that any organizations found to have engaged in proselytization will be punished.

This is not a new campaign, but rather the continuation of a pattern of persecution and repression perpetuated by laws such as the apostasy provisions and the systemic lack of enforcement of the rights contained in Afghanistan's own constitution. In fact, OFWI has obtained copies of the arrest and execution warrants issued by state and religious authorities in a number of cases before the broadcast. The following are only some of the cases that have taken place in recent years and that have been brought to our attention. Most of the individuals involved are now in third countries.

Obaidullah (Place of Birth: Kapisa; UNHCR Ref #: 07IND00956) received a letter from the local mosque which demanded that he appear before the religious leaders of the mosque and declare publicly that he was cheated by Christians into converting and that he repents and returns to Islam. If he failed to do so, he would be punished directly or delivered to the Islamic court to be executed. He fled and is in India.

Ghafar's (Place of Birth: Kabul; UNHCR Ref #: 09C03153) father was a Christian. He was killed and the family's house set on fire by Mujahideen groups in the 1990s. After his father's death, Ghafar and the rest of his family escaped to Iran where they made every effort to keep their Christianity secret. When the Karzai government came to power, Ghafar's mother and brother decided to return to Afghanistan where his brother, Satar, soon disappeared. His mother states that Satar was kidnapped by people calling him a "pagan" and "infidel" and threatening that it was "time to remove your dirty name from the surface of the earth". He has not been heard of since and his body has not been found. In the meantime Ghafar himself also left Iran where he experienced persecution and is now in India.

Bibi Zahra (Place of birth: Sare Pul; UNHCR Ref #: 10C00563) was arrested by Afghan police who demanded she pay them $3,000 USD. The police intended to deliver her to the Islamic court to be sentenced to life in prison for leaving Islam and to force her to reveal the names and details of all Christian fellowships and believers that she knew in Afghanistan. She was released and told to leave the area after giving the police $1,300 USD (an enormous sum for Afghans) as a bribe. Through further bribes she was able to leave the country with her three small daughters and is now in India.

Ghulam Sarwar Haidari (Place of birth: Kabul; Afghan Passport #: OA 240872) was arrested and beaten by police in Kabul City. After he was released against money, his relatives beat him and sought to deliver him to the police. He escaped and is now in India.

Plight of Afghan Refugee Claimants Abroad

Even those converts who are able to flee from the country are not safe from persecution. Afghan authorities routinely harass and threaten converts from Islam who have found refuge abroad. In one such case, Abdul (Place of birth: Ghazni; UNHCR Ref #: 07C01139) and another Afghan Christian were detained by the Afghan Embassy in New Delhi in 2009. The embassy had obtained photos of all Afghan Christians who lived in New Delhi and the two were detained when they attended at the embassy to try to obtain a letter for a little girl who needed a kidney transplant. They were forced to tell embassy officials that they were not Christians and that they had lied to the UNHCR office about being Christians, after which they were released.

Moreover, converts who apply for refugee status are placed in an extremely vulnerable position as a failed application and subsequent deportation will alert the Afghan government of their conversion and places them in extreme danger of persecution or even death upon their return. What follows are only two examples of the profound insecurity faced by Afghan refugee claimants, who must live in constant fear of being deported to face added persecution.

Shahvalay's (Place of birth: Kunduz; UNHCR ref #: 786-10C06903) uncle and cousins tried to kill him in the year 2006. He fled the country but his case was rejected by the UNHCR, after which he was deported to Afghanistan. He was arrested at the Kabul airport on his return, his money was taken from him, and he was then released. He was in Kabul for a time during which he faced persecution and eluded attempts by the police to arrest him until he was finally forced to flee once again. He is now in Azerbaijan.

Salim's (Place of birth: Ghazni; UNHCR Ref #: 08C00014) father sought to deliver him to the police because of his conversion so he fled the country but was deported back to Afghanistan when his case was rejected by the UNHCR. He was followed by police and had to constantly move around from province to province until he was finally arrested. After the authorities forced him to divorce his wife and pay 8,000 Afghani he was released but a warrant for his arrest and execution remain.

Women in Afghanistan

After decades of war and conflict, women and children have been left an overlooked and marginalized segment of the population. Since the demise of the Taliban, some advances have been made, but serious problems remain and Afghan women and girls remain much worse off than before the Taliban emerged and face growing threats from the re-emergence of conservative forces in Afghan politics. Despite the vast store of wisdom that women could bring to the issues in Afghanistan, they continue to be marginalized, treated as irrelevant, and in many cases horribly abused.

Once again, Afghan law and international law provide theoretical rights for women. Article 22 of the Constitution, for instance, states:

> Any kind of discrimination and distinction between citizens of Afghanistan shall be forbidden. The citizens of Afghanistan, *man and woman, have equal rights and duties before the law.* (Emphasis added)

Afghanistan is also a signatory to the *Convention on the Elimination of All Forms of Discrimination Against Women* (CEDAW) which it ratified March 5, 2003. However, the Afghan government has failed to provide meaningful guarantees for these rights. Despite the passage of the 2009 law on *Elimination of Violence Against Women* in response to domestic and international pressure, a report released by the United Nations in November 2011 reports that the actual enforcement of the provisions by Afghan officials was "limited" at best and that "most incidents are unreported."[10] Moreover, the Afghan government has taken several troubling steps that directly

One Free World International

Rev. El Shafic, Founder and President of One Free World International, meets in post-Taliban Afghanistan with Afghan women who are victims of human rights abuses, including spousal abuse and forced marriages.

contradict the principles of equality and dignity contained in the above provisions and that further threaten the status of women in Afghanistan.

1. The Shi'a Personal Status Law

On July 27, 2009, at the same time as the passage of the aforementioned *Elimination of Violence Against Women Law,* the government of Afghanistan passed an essentially contradictory piece of legislation in the *Shi'a Personal Status* law. As it only applies to the minority Shi'a population, this personal status law is both a violation of women's rights *and* religious freedom, as it unjustly discriminates between women on the basis of religion. While it will be acknowledged that the law was modified from the original proposal under heavy international pressure, it still contains provisions that are of serious concern and clearly violate the Afghan constitution, international human rights law, and Afghanistan's express international commitments and obligations.

In fact, despite the amendments, the law as passed is not appreciably better than the original, as it perpetuates and condones the dehumanization and abuse of Afghan women. A provision requiring wives to have sexual relations with their husbands at a minimum every four days was replaced with a provision that allows husbands to withhold basic necessities, including food, if their wives refuse to meet their sexual demands. With this provision the law sanctions a form of marital rape, since a threat to withdraw the necessities of life constitutes coercion and effectively voids any consent a wife may give, leaving Shi'a women at the complete mercy of the sexual whims and demands of their husbands. The law also retains many of the other discriminatory provisions of the original draft, including exclusive male custody and continued restrictions on the mobility of women outside the home.[11]

2. Ulema Council Restrictions on Status of Women Endorsed by President Karzai

In a troubling recent development, President Karzai has endorsed a highly restrictive 'code of conduct' for women issued on March 2, 2012 by Afghanistan's Ulema Council,[12] a very powerful (and government-funded) religious advisory body composed of the state's top Muslim clerics. In a statement on March 6, two days before International Women's Day, President Karzai denied that the guidelines "propose any limitations" on Afghan women, but that they merely "announced Islamic principles and values…in accordance with a Shari'a view of our country, which all Muslims and Afghans are committed to."[13]

However, the provisions of the 'code' are in clear violation of both the Afghan constitutional principles of equality outlined above and international human rights standards—and represent a major step backwards for women in Afghanistan. The declaration contains a clear statement that "men are fundamental and women are secondary,"[14] along with a prohibition to interact with males in "social situations" including the office and school—a provision that would seriously curtail women's ability to participate in society outside the home. Women are also called upon to "[avoid] travel without a [male companion]," and the guidelines also forbid the beating of women only in cases where there is no "Shariah-compliant reason." Indeed, women's rights groups in Afghanistan are warning that these provisions are reminiscent of the position of the Taliban and that President Karzai's endorsement is a worrisome sign that the Afghan government is using the rights of women as a pawn in a political game.

Boy Play—The "Bacha Bazi"

Bacha bazi, or boy play, is an ancient custom that goes back centuries and possibly thousands of years in Afghanistan. It was banned under the Taliban regime but has been revived, particularly in the northern regions, since the Taliban's demise and attendant increase in certain freedoms. The practice has been brought to light in the western media by several international news agencies, including a special investigative report by PBS's

One Free World International

Fadin (age 14) has been kidnapped twice. He was forced to wear women's clothing and dance and was raped by men and beaten. Unlike many others, he is one of the lucky ones; the last time this happened, his father was alerted to it and rescued him.

Frontline.[15] It has been condemned by Islamic scholars as un-Islamic and as a form of sexual slavery by the United Nations Under-Secretary-General, Radhika Coomaraswamy, yet it is re-surfacing.

In this deplorable custom, powerful men take poor and vulnerable boys into their "protection", sometimes with the approval of the boys' families. They promise to train them or give them work and prepare them for a better life. In actuality, the boys are taken into a form of sexual slavery from which they have no escape. Their masters teach them to entertain their friends by dressing in women's clothing and dancing seductively in front of all-male audiences. Masters compete among each other for prestige and social rank for having the best boys. At the end of the evening the boys are often shared for sexual favours or bought and sold among masters with such events often ending in assault and rape. *Bacha bazi* boys are commonly threatened and assaulted and have been killed as a result of disputes between the men involved or for attempting to escape.

There is no way around the conclusion that this practice is slavery. The boys taken into this life are teens and children as young as 11 and sometimes much younger. They are poor and vulnerable, often orphans or street-children or from poor or abusive families. The boys are lured, usually by rich, powerful men, under false pretences of protection, education or training, and a better life. The true nature of the relationship is not revealed until it is too late. The boys have no choice in entering this life-style and once they are in it they do not have the choice to leave. Even if they succeed in leaving they are burdened with the stigma of having been *bacha bazi*. One of the most heart-wrenching aspects of this despicable practice is that often when the boys grow up they in turn take boys of their own, condemning generations of Afghan boys to a vicious cycle of sexual abuse and slavery.

The failure by the Afghan government to put an end to this deplorable practice is a grievous violation of its international human rights obligations and of its basic duty toward its own citizens. Children are Afghanistan's future. Yet they are the most vulnerable of all and need the protection and guidance of their parents, communities, and the state. As President Karzai stated in characterizing as a crime against humanity the reported execution by the Taliban of a 7-year-old boy as a spy, "A 7-year-old boy cannot be anything but a 7-year-old boy."[16] Certainly the same applies to young boys whose dignity, future, and too often their very lives are stolen from them by powerful men in pursuit of power, prestige, and sexual gratification. If the people of Afghanistan and the leadership of the country cannot protect its children, it has no future.

IV. RECOMMENDATIONS FOR U.S. FOREIGN POLICY IN AFGHANISTAN AND PAKISTAN

The eyes of the world are on the United States and its actions in the Middle East and South Asia. The United States' position as a global leader and the very integrity of the principles on which its foreign policy purports to be based demand immediate and substantive action to address the abuses outlined above. Despite the fact that President Obama stood in Cairo in June 2009 and affirmed that, "[f]reedom of religion is central to the ability of peoples to live together,"[17] religious freedom has often been marginalized and subordinated to other considerations in the formulation and implementation of U.S. foreign policy toward Pakistan and Afghanistan. This trend cannot be allowed to continue as inaction in this area will effectively undermine U.S. moral authority in its dealings with other states.

Moreover, violations of religious freedom are often at the root or at least central to regional instability and anti-democratic trends. As a result, any U.S. foreign policy efforts aimed at promoting democracy, social stability, peace, and security without taking into account the issue of religious freedom effectively ignore one of the fundamental sources of the very problem they are seeking to address and are, therefore, destined to fail. Unless meaningful steps are taken to prioritize religious freedom in U.S. relations with Pakistan and Afghanistan, U.S. foreign policy in these very religious states will not only be highly ineffective, but will also risk exacerbating tensions and insecurity in the region.

In these societies where the role of religion as a foundational source of individual identity is particularly heightened and the acknowledged organizing principle of society itself, the absence of religious freedom forces individuals to choose between living as second class citizens, being denied the right to participate in the full benefits of society, or denying their most deeply held beliefs in order to participate in the public sphere. This is an untenable choice, and history and experience clearly demonstrate that societies where religious freedom is denied are incapable of sustaining meaningful democratic institutions and are highly susceptible to both internal and external conflict.

Designate as "Country of Particular Concern" (CPC)—and Adopt Substantive Measures

A source of great concern is the failure by the State Department to designate either Pakistan or Afghanistan as "Countries of Particular Concern". According to the *International Religious Freedom Act,* a "country of particular concern" is one that "has engaged in or *tolerated* particularly severe violations of religious freedom" (emphasis added).[18] In light of the deplorable state of religious freedom (and human rights more generally) in both Afghanistan and Pakistan, as I have outlined, it is difficult to conceive of any reason why each of these countries would not meet this threshold. The United States must not sacrifice human rights for the sake of geopolitical considerations. The credibility of the United States' commitment to religious freedom can only be maintained if it is willing to apply the CPC designation to its allies as well as to its enemies.

Such a designation, however, must be more than symbolic, and the United States must use all foreign policy tools at its disposal to address the violations described in this statement and ensure that both governments in question take the necessary steps to ensure long-term protection of the rights of religious minorities, women, and children. As history has shown, diplomatic engagement and political dialogue—however sustained and constructive—are often insufficient. In order for U.S. diplomatic engagement to be effective in both of these countries, it must be backed by a demonstrable commitment to take substantive policy action in response to violations. If either of these governments is not willing to respond positively to the United States' representations, it must not continue its relationship with that country on a "business-as-usual" basis but be willing to disengage and make the resumption of normal relations conditional on measurable progress in the area of religious freedom.

The purpose behind the recommended actions is not simply to punish violating states and voice the United States' outrage at the behaviour in question. Punishment is not an end in itself but a means to achieve the ultimate purpose of seeing Pakistan and Afghanistan take positive steps toward the protection of religious freedom by providing them with a real incentive to change their behaviour. In Pakistan, for instance, the United States must apply substantive policy measures to exert pressure on the government to repeal its blasphemy laws, while in Afghanistan such targeted measures must be used to compel the Western-backed government to desist from its officially-sanctioned policy of pursuing converts from Islam. These examples are certainly not an exhaustive list of the issues that must be addressed in the pursuit of real religious freedom, but one must begin somewhere and these items represent areas in which the United States must begin to move beyond mere rhetoric and take real, substantive action.

Link U.S. Aid to Human Rights with Clear Reference to Religious Freedom

Perhaps the most effective way for the United States to encourage both these governments to address the state of religious freedom is to create an explicit link between that country's respect for freedom of religion and its eligibility to receive U.S. aid. Given the magnitude of U.S. contributions to each of these countries, international aid is perhaps the United States' most powerful means of exerting pressure on states that refuse to respond positively to its diplomatic efforts in matters relating to religious freedom. Moreover, the resumption of aid payments (or the return to previous levels) must be made conditional on the attainment of achievable yet substantial targets in terms of protecting freedom of religion—and human rights more generally. This approach will provide an incentive for violating states to take measurable steps while, at the same time, demonstrating the United States' unwavering commitment to religious freedom as a vital component of its foreign policy.

The legislative authority for such an explicit link between aid and religious freedom already exists within *IRFA* and the *Foreign Assistance Act* of 1961. Section 2(b) of *IRFA* clearly states that it "shall be the policy of the United States ... to seek to channel United States security and development assistance to governments other than those found to be engaged in gross violations of freedom of religion."[19] Moreover, section 405(a) of *IRFA*[20] empowers the President to authorize the "withdrawal, limitation, or suspension of" both "development assistance" (paragraph 9) and "security assistance" (paragraph 11) in accordance with the *Foreign Assistance Act*. Section 116(a) of the *Foreign Assistance Act* further states that "no assistance may be provided under this part to the government of any country which engages in a consistent pattern of gross violations of international human rights,"[21] including "particularly severe violations of religious freedom."[22]

If the United States is serious about its commitment to religious freedom, it must take action based on this authority given to it by Congress to compel these countries to undertake positive change or face serious consequences. As I prepare this statement, however, there are troubling reports that the current administration is planning on effectively sidestepping the provisions of the *2012 Consolidated Appropriations Act*,[23] which required that military aid to Egypt be contingent on the latter "implementing policies to protect freedom of expression, association, and religion, and due process of law."[24] By invoking the "national security" provision of the *Act*,[25] the administration is effectively validating the human rights violations of the transitional military council in Egypt—which I documented during my testimony before the U.S. House Subcommittee on Africa, Global Health, and Human Rights[26]—and signalling that relations will proceed on a 'business-as-usual' basis.

While these provisions relate specifically to Egypt, such an action would be a clear message to all governments, including those of Pakistan and Afghanistan, that the United States is not committed to human rights (and religious freedom more specifically). By continuing to provide unconditional assistance to a military and security establishment that not only refuses to live up to its basic responsibilities toward Egypt's most vulnerable citizens, but that is also responsible for *directly* attacking and murdering members of the Christian minority, the United States will show the world that it is prepared to subordinate religious freedom and human rights to self-interested political considerations.

1. Pakistan: Abolishing Blasphemy Laws and Ending Impunity for Rape and Slavery

The United States government has allocated nearly $3 billion of aid for Pakistan as part of its 2012 budget, including over $1.5 billion of security sector assistance (not including counter-terrorism).[27] The United States cannot continue to provide essentially 'blank cheques' to a government and security establishment that not only turns a blind eye to the rape and slavery occurring within its borders, but also imprisons its own citizens under threat of the death sentence simply because of their beliefs—under the guise of an unconscionable 'blasphemy' law. While Pakistan is a valuable U.S. ally in the region, American interests cannot be purchased at the cost of the basic human rights of Pakistani minorities. The United States has a responsibility to make the continuation of its substantial aid program in Pakistan conditional on the repeal of the blasphemy laws and on measurable progress toward ending impunity for rapists of minority women and those who enslave minority families in labour camps.

2. Afghanistan: Halting Persecution of Converts and Respecting Women and Children

The United States government has allocated over $3.2 billion of aid for Afghanistan as part of its 2012 budget, of which less than 8% is to be directed to "rule of law and human rights."[28] There is no question that the United States has a responsibility to assist Afghanistan during this period of transition. However, the United States must use the influence it has by virtue of providing an amount of aid roughly equivalent to 18% of Afghanistan's total GDP[29] to demand that the government immediately cease the officially sanctioned persecution of converts and begin respecting the rights of women and children. When the United States stands by while one of the governments it supports (both politically and financially) systematically violates the human rights of its citizens, it becomes complicit in these crimes. U.S. officials must demand accountability from their Afghan counterparts as to how the aid money is being used, and they must make clear to the Afghani government that U.S. support is conditional on progress on the human rights issues outlined above.

Link U.S. Trade to Human Rights with Clear Reference to Religious Freedom

The United States must not carry on 'business-as-usual' aid relationships with Pakistan and Afghanistan so long as their respective governments refuse to take substantive steps to address the abuses occurring within their borders. However, both countries have significant trading relationships with the United States. In 2011, the United States exported over $2 billion of goods to Pakistan, and in turn imported just under $4 billion of Pakistani goods.[30] In 2010, the United States accounted for 15.9% of total Pakistani exports and for just under 10% of Pakistan's total bilateral trade.[31] While Afghanistan was not a significant source of American imports, the United States exported nearly $3 billion of goods to Afghanistan in 2011.[32] As of 2010, the Unites States is Afghanistan's largest trading partner, accounting for nearly 1/3 of all Afghani bilateral trade.[33]

These economic relationships provide the United States with a significant avenue for influence over both the Pakistani and Afghani governments if they fail to make the necessary changes to ensure the protection of religious minorities. If other policy options to this end fail, the United States must curtail its trade relationship with these states. Any government that persistently refuses to protect the human rights of its citizens must not be able to count on a business relationship with the United States with 'no strings attached'—as this would amount to an outright abdication of the United States' professed commitment to religious freedom in the world.

At the same time, the Unites States government must identify specific steps relating to religious freedom that would lead to a resumption (or continuation, as the case may be) of normal economic relations. By setting achievable yet substantial targets for progress in the area of religious freedom in these countries, the United States can both promote positive and sincere engagement and ensure that the governments in question demonstrate a real commitment to achieve measurable progress toward the protection of fundamental human rights for all their citizens. Such an approach will help prevent the perception of the measures as heavy-handed and overly punitive, while also providing a positive incentive for each respective government to make measurable changes to its behaviour.

Build Multilateral Partnerships

Based on my experience, I believe that a major hindrance to U.S. efforts to promote religious freedom in these countries is the strong reaction against perceived U.S. unilateralism. While bilateral engagement is vitally important—and indeed most of our recommendations relate to U.S. bilateral relations—in order to enhance the effectiveness and legitimacy of its policies, the United States must be willing to create partnerships with like-minded states and to strengthen its engagements with multilateral initiatives on these issues. The importance of such multilateral engagement was emphasized by Congress in *IRFA*, which states, in section 2:

> (b) It shall be the policy of the United States …:
>
> …(4) To work with foreign governments that affirm and protect religious freedom, in order to develop multilateral documents and initiatives to combat violations of religious freedom and promote the right to religious freedom abroad.

To this end, the United States must broaden its partnerships with regional organizations and countries such as Canada who share the same commitment to global religious freedom. Working with initiatives such as the Canadian government's newly-announced Office of Religious Freedom, for example, will help create a coalition of states that will be more effective than the United States can be working alone.

Moreover, in order to ensure that it has the necessary moral authority to promote religious freedom around the world, it is vital that the United States strengthen its engagement with other human rights initiatives and instruments. As has already been noted above, religious freedom is intimately inter-connected with all other human rights; therefore, any efforts to promote religious freedom while overlooking other key rights will be incomplete at best. Additionally, U.S. actions will be seen as more legitimate—and not driven by narrow interests—if its efforts to uphold global religious freedom are accompanied by corresponding efforts on behalf of human rights more broadly.

Assist Vulnerable Refugees

Despite all other efforts, and certainly until respect for human rights is accepted as a fundamental value of these countries, victims of religious persecution may have no option but to flee their homes to secure their safety. During the course of our work on behalf of victims of persecution in Pakistan and Afghanistan, I have observed the importance of refugee protection as a safety net where all other efforts have failed. As the case of Neeha I discussed previously illustrates, the decision to grant asylum can mean the difference between life and death. Moreover, as I have outlined above, Afghan converts from Islam whose asylum claims are rejected face the certainty of persecution and the very real possibility of arrest (and even execution) upon their return—as the failed asylum claim serves to alert the government of their conversion.

It is critical, therefore, that the United States take steps to ensure that its refugee protection system is up to the task of providing this life-saving solution to victims of religious persecution. This means ensuring that decision-makers and immigration officers are knowledgeable about issues around religious persecution and given the necessary resources so that legitimate cases can be determined in a timely fashion. Moreover, U.S. immigration policy must reflect the reality that religious minorities from Pakistan and Afghanistan are not safe even if they flee to the surrounding countries, where their religious beliefs and practices render them all but as vulnerable as in their country of origin.

V. CONCLUSION

Every member of the international community bears a sacred trust to uphold fundamental human rights. There is no right more fundamental to human dignity and to truly free and inclusive societies than freedom of religion. In light of the appalling abuses of this basic right occurring throughout the world today, no country, the United States included, can say that it has fulfilled its duty to protect religious freedom and the vulnerable minorities to whom this freedom is denied.

While I commend the United States for publicly stating its commitment to religious freedom—and for enshrining that commitment in law—statements of concern and condemnation must be followed up with substance and action. Will it continue to treat religious freedom as an afterthought in its foreign policy and risk its moral authority as a leader on this issue, or will the United States government renew its commitment to global freedom of religion and take an unwavering stand on behalf of vulnerable minorities?

To retain its moral authority in global affairs, the United States cannot sacrifice for the sake of political expediency the basic principles of human rights and fundamental freedoms which it asserts as the foundation for its own domestic values. Standing by while vulnerable minorities, women, and children are abused within the borders of its allies is simply not an option if the United States wishes to preserve its standing as a leader on the world stage.

The United States is facing a choice as to how its influence will help shape the future of two countries that, while purporting to be democracies, have thus far failed to uphold the basic human rights of their citizens. It has a unique opportunity to assist both Pakistan and Afghanistan to pursue the path of freedom and the rule of law, but inaction at this crucial juncture could have devastating consequences not only for the region's religious minorities, but also for global stability and, therefore, the security of the

United States itself. At this pivotal moment in history, will the United States choose to be part of the problem or the heart of the solution?

Rev. Majed El Shafie was detained and severely tortured by authorities in his native Egypt when he converted from Islam to Christianity and began pursuing equal rights for Egyptian Christians. After he was sentenced to death, he was able to escape from Egypt and finally settled in Canada where he established One Free World International (OFWI) to share a message of freedom, hope, and tolerance for religious differences and to promote human rights. OFWI is based in Toronto, Canada, and advocates on behalf of individual victims and communities directly with governments both in countries of concern and in the West and assists religious minorities in practical ways through humanitarian aid. More information about Rev. El Shafie and the work of One Free World International is available at www.onefreeworldinternational.org.

SUMMARY OF RECOMMENDATIONS

In order to live up to its stated commitment to global religious freedom, the United States must adopt a more comprehensive and proactive approach to this issue, particularly in relation to Pakistan and Afghanistan. In Pakistan religious minorities like Christians, Hindus, and Ahmadi Muslims are treated as second-class citizens, vulnerable to vague and draconian Blasphemy Laws, rape and forced conversion of women, and indentured servitude. In Afghanistan converts from Islam face death for apostasy while women and children are vulnerable to abusive laws and traditional practices.

Standing by is not an option. The United States has a unique opportunity to assist both Pakistan and Afghanistan to pursue the path of freedom and the rule of law, but inaction at this crucial juncture could have devastating consequences not only for the region's religious minorities, but also for global stability and, therefore, the security of the United States itself. The United

States' position as a global leader and the very integrity of the principles on which it purports to base its domestic values and foreign policy are at stake.

Religious Freedom and Foreign Policy

1. foreign policy must be based on the premise that religious freedom is not only a humanitarian concern, but also a *pre-requisite* for stable democracy, social stability, and global security

2. a comprehensive and proactive approach to religious freedom must be part of long-term foreign policy

   - religious freedom initiatives must be fully implemented into long-term policy and not restricted to *ad hoc* interventions in individual cases

   - proactive in promotion of religious freedom as a vital foreign policy interests, and not merely reactive measures, is needed

   - religious freedom must be prioritized in and integrated into the mainstream of foreign policy as provided for in the U.S. by the *International Religious Freedom Act*

Recommendations for U.S. Foreign Policy in Afghanistan and Pakistan

1. designate both Pakistan and Afghanistan as *CPCs* and follow through on this designation by enacting *substantive policy measures* when they are unresponsive to dialogue

2. U.S. foreign *aid* (both general aid and security assistance) must be explicitly linked to religious freedom and conditional on substantive progress in this area

3. the U.S. must not continue 'business-as-usual' economic relations with these states, and must be willing to curtail its *trade* relationships in the absence of positive progress on human rights

4. the U.S. must build *multilateral partnerships* with like-minded states and international bodies to enhance the effectiveness of its policies and counter perceptions of unilateralism

5. the U.S. must ensure that its *refugee protection* system provides an effective remedy of last resort for legitimate refugees who will be persecuted if deported

Appendix D

Submission by One Free World International for the
Parliamentary Inquiry into Antisemitism in Canada to the
Canadian Parliamentary Coalition of Combat Antisemitism
August 31, 2009

I. INTRODUCTION

Antisemitism is an abhorrent attitude that has led to untold suffering throughout the ages. It dehumanizes the Jewish people thus justifying discrimination, exploitation, abuse, and even murder. Its inevitable end is attempted destruction of the Jewish people as in the Nazi Holocaust.

While we would like to believe that antisemitism is only a historical issue and no longer relevant, it is on the increase in Canada and worldwide. It continues to surface in traditional ways with open verbal, symbolic, or physical attacks against Jewish individuals or symbols. On the other hand, a new, contemporary antisemitism couches itself in the cloak of anti-zionism, spun as "legitimate" criticism of the State of Israel.

The frame of reference for this Parliamentary Inquiry relates to antisemitism in Canada. However, antisemitism in Canada today cannot be viewed in isolation from its broader historical and international context or from its relationship to the treatment of other religious minorities around the world. Since most contributors to this Inquiry are expected to focus on Canada, the present submissions will focus on the broader view, relating it to the Canadian context. More information about the incidents mentioned herein can be obtained by contacting OFWI.

II. ABOUT ONE FREE WORLD INTERNATIONAL (OFWI)

Reverend Majed El Shafie, President and Founder of OFWI, was born in Egypt to a prominent Muslim family of judges and lawyers. He was detained and severely tortured by Egyptian authorities after he converted to Christianity and began advocating equal rights for Egyptian Christians. Sentenced to death, he fled Egypt by way of Israel and settled in Canada in 2002, establishing OFWI to share a message of freedom, hope, and tolerance for religious differences and to promote human rights in this area through advocacy and public education.

Rev. El Shafie has testified twice before the Subcommittee on International Human Rights of the Standing Committee on Foreign Affairs and International Development and has provided expert reports or expert testimony in numerous refugee proceedings in Canada and the United States. OFWI supports religious freedom without regard to the victims' religion or creed. Accordingly, it also stands against antisemitism and has organized several inter-faith events in cooperation with B'nai Brith Canada. It has an extensive network of local sources in Muslim and communist countries and cooperates with other human rights observers and organizations. More information is available on the OFWI website at www.onefreeworldinternational.org.

III. ANTISEMITISM: HISTORY

The history of antisemitism and its culmination in the horrors of the Holocaust are well-known. Yet we must not take such knowledge for granted, but must continue to tell the story in order to educate new generations and so we would not forget or become complacent.

From the exile of the Jews by the Romans after the destruction of the Temple in Jerusalem to the Spanish Inquisition and from the pogroms of Russia to the Edicts of Expulsion (Spain and England, among others) and finally to the horrors of the Nazi gas chambers, Jews have been harassed, discriminated, oppressed, persecuted, and killed, simply because they were Jews. The sixty-odd years since the end of the Second World War and the establishment of the State of Israel have provided the Jewish people with a rare moment of reprieve from the constant onslaught of antisemitism. *- except in the Middle East and North Africa.* Yet even that precarious respite has begun to show distinct signs of running out, especially over the last decade.

Canada is not free from the stain of antisemitism despite our history of openness, tolerance, and welcoming immigration. His- *The Nazis had a lot of allies and influence in the Arab world, and the effect of Nazi propaganda continues there.* torically we must acknowledge, for example, a strong climate of antisemitism in the period before and into the Second World War. Canada's immigration policy was extremely restrictive toward Jewish immigrants and refugees. Even in 1939 when the nature of Nazi policies was already apparent, Canada sent over 900 Jewish refugees on the St. Louis ship back to Europe where many perished in Nazi death camps.

As the full horrors of the Holocaust were revealed in the aftermath of the Second World War, entire generations were traumatized by the evidence of human capacity for evil against their fellow human beings and swore, "Never again".

IV. ANTISEMITISM: CONTEMPORARY MANIFESTATIONS AND NATURE

While there are no Nazi death camps today, traditional antisemitism persists. Fascism of the 20th century has given way to a self-righteous, nefarious antisemitism from the left of the political spectrum which shares the field with various forms of neo-fascist ideology on the extreme right. Manifestations include attacks on Jewish individuals, businesses, synagogues, schools, and other identifiable Jewish targets. In Europe Jewish cemeteries are defaced and in Paris a young Jewish man was kidnapped and brutally tortured for 24 days before being killed in unimaginable horror by 23 people with the indirect involvement or wilful blindness of dozens of others. Closer to home, synagogues and schools have been vandalized or firebombed from Montreal and Quebec City to Kelowna, while university students conceal their Jewish identity to avoid harassment and intimidation on campus amid hostile protests and "academic" conferences that are little more than anti-Israel propaganda sessions.

Contemporary antisemitism typically masquerades as anti-zionism. Various examples include for example op-eds and editorials harshly critical of Israel; comparisons between Israeli policies and apartheid or Nazi Germany; biased and even falsified news reporting in such unexpected places as Sweden, with the support of the government moreover; Israeli athletes and sports teams excluded from sporting events or welcomed with Nazi greetings; vicious anti-Israel demonstrations; and calls for boycotts. In Canada, only a few weeks ago the United Church of Canada rejected a resolution mandating a concerted boycott of Israel, but passed one encouraging individual groups and churches to examine the issue and take appropriate measures.

There is no question that Israel can and should be evaluated and critiqued on its policies just like any other state as long as such criticism is based on facts and truth. Anti-zionism, however, goes beyond legitimate criticism and transfers antisemitic thought patterns from the people to the state. Where it is morally reprehensible to question the right of Jews to exist as individuals and as a people, questioning the legitimacy of the State of Israel or its right to defend itself seems superficially acceptable and does not attract the same censure. Yet the same antisemitic logic operates as is plainly obvious if one tries to apply the same critiques to other states. Consequently, antisemitism in this paper is understood to include anti-zionism.

The rise of contemporary antisemitism is of particular concern because of its ready acceptance in academia, the media, and among the political classes in many countries and the influence these have on the mainstream. Antisemitism in academia benefits from the air of legitimacy associated with scholarship and leaves an indelible impact on future generations of decision-makers causing damage far beyond proportion. In the news media anti-semitism directly influences the "man-in-the-street". Yet media "objectivity" has somehow come to mean, not the dispassionate reporting of facts, but presenting a balance between competing positions, regardless of their relative merits or moral strengths. This has resulted in imputing moral equivalence to Israel's actions of self-defence and those of terrorists attacking innocent Israelis, which can only be described as bias. Finally, antisemitism in political classes leads to antisemitism in the community being downplayed, anti-Israel slugfests like the Durban conference on racism, and blatantly one-sided resolutions at the United Nations.

Another concern is the increasingly public nature of antisemitic acts and the recurrent theme of onlookers doing nothing to protect victims. To the extent that the general public is indifferent or condones antisemitic actions even after decades of public education campaigns about human rights and the horrors to which antisemitism can lead, the future is bleak indeed.

V. ANTISEMITISM AND OTHER RELIGIOUS MINORITIES

While the effect of antisemitism on Jews as fellow human beings is sufficient reason to be concerned, it is not the only reason. Despite increases in antisemitism, historically speaking Jews still live and worship relatively freely in the West and have some safety in the protection of the State of Israel. On the other hand, human nature has not changed, as evidenced in the genocide of Rwanda in the 1990s. In the 21st century, black African Muslims in Darfur are brutalized by their Arab Muslim countrymen, converts from

Islam are pursued by the death penalty across the Muslim world, and any Christians discovered in North Korea and unregistered church leaders in China are imprisoned, put to forced labor, and often tortured, particularly in the former.

These are only a minuscule sampling of events taking place today around the world, or even in the countries mentioned. But what do they have to do with antisemitism in Canada? Nothing on the surface, and yet everything. Because where human beings think little or nothing of oppressing their fellow human beings, whether because of the colour of their skin or their religious beliefs or rites, the identity of the victim matters little. In fact, the only reason we do not hear of Jews persecuted in many of these countries despite rampant antisemitism is that any Jewish community that may once have existed is now either virtually or actually non-existent. The following examples demonstrate how antisemitism and per-secution of other religious minorities coexist.

Despite a peace agreement with Israel committing it to abstain from hostile propaganda or incitement, Egypt's state-run media are full of grossly antisemitic and anti-Israel political cartoons, editorials, and television programs; school textbooks omit Israel on maps and declare that Israel remains the enemy and that war can break at any moment; and authorities close their eyes to ter-rorists smuggling weapons to Gaza. At the same time, Christians, Bahá'í's and others are discriminated and fear forcible conver-sion, imprisonment, and possible torture, while converts are often tortured or killed even by their own family-members.

The President of Iran rants against Israel threatening its destruc-tion, pursues nuclear weapons, and Iranian Jews, and often Bahá'í's, are charged with spying for Israel. Meanwhile Iranian Christians and Bahá'í's are frequently arrested and held without charge, and converts are tortured to extract the names of other converts or information about house churches.

In Pakistan, despite the absence of any apparent Jewish community, antisemitism and anti-zionism are widespread. In the meantime, impoverished Christians are lured into enslavement in this country where a two-year old Christian girl can be raped because her father refuses to convert to Islam. Christians, Hindus, and others are killed arbitrarily with vague and draconian Blasphemy Laws serving as pretext, and Ahmadis, considered heretics, are prohibited under threat of criminal sanction by anti-Ahmadi laws from presenting themselves as Muslims or publicly observing rites.

Saudi Arabia officially prohibits entry to Israelis or those with Israeli stamps in their passports and unofficially bans Jews. In 2005 a teacher who had spoken positively about Jews and the Bible was sentenced to almost three and a half years in penitentiary and 750 lashes before OFWI intervention led to his release. At the same time, the Muslim Shi'a minority faces discrimination, all public non-Muslim religious practice is forbidden and religious police periodically raid even the private religious gatherings of foreigners imprisoning participants and confiscating Bibles.

Problems with "media objectivity" apply here as much as to antisemitism. For example, in a recent Canadian news report, an American-born girl who fled home claiming her father had threatened to kill her for converting from Islam to Christianity was characterized as a normal rebellious teenager afraid of "punishment", omitting any mention of death threats. Such attitudes and reporting make any resolution of the human rights issues involved impossible as the first victim of this false objectivity is the truth. However, the real victims of such distortion are Jews and others whose religious beliefs make them a target.

Just like in Nazi Germany, wherever antisemitism flourishes other religious or ethnic minorities, the disabled, homosexuals, and others eventually face persecution, and other basic human rights, such as women's rights, freedom of expression, etc., are or soon will be threatened. If left unchecked such attitudes and oppression will spread like poison and affect Jews and other minorities alike worldwide. Even if they do not result in wide-scale antisemitism or anti-religious behaviours in Canada, the potential for a cataclysmic and costly world war to protect our freedoms is very real and the results not a foregone conclusion. As a result, it is our responsibility to speak out, to come to the aid of victims, and to ensure that such attitudes are not permitted to flourish in Canada or anywhere else in the world.

VI. CONCLUSION AND RECOMMENDATIONS

History teaches us that if we do not remember and learn from our history we are destined to repeat our mistakes. There is perhaps no lesson more important than that of antisemitism, the Holocaust, and genocide, yet we do not seem to learn this lesson. The Rwandan genocide, the greatest example of an entirely avoidable evil since the Holocaust, took place despite clear warning signs that the world simply chose to ignore. In the meantime, antisemitism simmers.

If the rise of antisemitism is permitted to go unchecked, the result will be another holocaust more destructive, more barbaric, and more unthinkable than that unleashed by the Nazis in the 1930s and 1940s. The spirit of hatred and intolerance will not rest with the destruction of the Jewish state and elimination of all Jews, but will endanger all freedom-loving peoples.

We have plenty of laws in place to protect individuals and property from generic and antisemitic crimes. We do not need more laws or regulations. We need the political will to enforce those laws that already exist. We need leaders in and out of government with the moral strength to speak truth boldly, loudly, and clearly to those, individuals, governments, or media, who would hide behind false notions of political correctness, self-righteous politics whether of the extreme right or left, or the false cover of a disingenuous concept of anti-zionism. We must also encourage other governments to do the same, for example showing the Swedish government that it is possible to support freedom of the press while still condemning vile content. Finally, we must not be afraid to clearly state the connection where it exists between incidents such as the Paris torture case and extremist Islamic teachings.

If we do not speak out on behalf of the Jewish people and against antisemitism today, who will speak out tomorrow for the Christians, or Bahá'í's, Uyghur or Darfur Muslims, Tibetan Buddhists, or Ahmadis, to mention only a few? Antisemitism is everyone's issue and we must not be silent.

ENDNOTES

Preface

1. Mike Maslanik, Teresa Neumann, "Persecuted Muslim Convert to Christianity Urges Love and Forgiveness"; http://www.breakingchristiannews.com/articles/display_art.html?ID=1951; accessed January 23, 2012.

Chapter 2

1. Erick Stakelbeck, "Muslim Brotherhood: A Global Terrorist Influence, *CBN News;* http://www.cbn.com/cbnnews/world/2011/February/Muslim-Brotherhood-A-Global-Terrorist-Influence; accessed February 9, 2012.

2. http://www.international.gc.ca/world/embassies/factsheets/egypt-FS-en.pdf; accessed April 10, 2012.

3. http://www.acdi-cida.gc.ca/acdi-cida/ACDI-CIDA.nsf/Eng/JUD-124143925-R37; accessed April 10, 2012.

4. U.S. Department of State: Arab Republic of Egypt, March 19, 2012; http://www.state.gov/r/pa/ei/bgn/5309.htm#relations; accessed March 28, 2012.

5. Rhonda Spivak is editor of the online newspaper *The Winnipeg Jewish Review,* found at www.winnipegjewishreview.com

6. Lawrence Solomon, "Exodus from the Arab Spring," October 18, 2011; http://www.theglobeandmail.com/news/

opinions/opinion/exodus-from-the-arab-spring/article2200409/; accessed January 23, 2012. *Lawrence Solomon is a founder of Probe International, a Toronto-based think tank.*

Chapter 3

1. United States Commission on International Religious Freedom, 2011; http://www.uscirf.gov/component/content/article/25-east-asia/2091-countries-of-particular-concern-china.html; accessed May 15, 2012.

2. David Matas and David Kilgour, *Bloody Harvest* (Woodstock, ON: Seraphim Editions, 2009).

3. http://www.faluninfo.net/article/1216/; accessed April 10, 2012.

4. Hon. David Kilgour, J.D., October 3, 2010; Speech: Organ Pillaging, Ongoing Crime Against Humanity by Chinese Party-State; Remarks presented during the Conference of the International Society for Human Rights (ISHR) on Sept. 30, 2010 at the Palais des Nations, United Nations Complex in Geneva; http://chinaview.wordpress.com/2010/10/03/speech-organ-pillaging-ongoing-crime-against-humanity-by-chinese-party-state/#more-7956; accessed February 10, 2012.

5. Peter Beaumont, foreign affairs editor; guardian.co.uk, July 18, 2009; http://www.guardian.co.uk/world/2009/jul/18/china-falun-gong-crackdown; accessed February 10, 2012.

6. Stefan J. Bos, chief international correspondent, *Worthy News,* December 27, 2011; "China Crackdown on Christmas Celebrations of House Churches; http://www.christianpersecution.info/index.php?view=11137; accessed January 15, 2012.

7. Independent Chinese PEN Centre was founded in 2001 by a group of Chinese writers in exile and in China, which makes vigorous efforts to promote and defend the freedom of writing and publication and the free flow of information in China and who are deeply concerned about the state of civil society and open discourse there. http://www.chinesepen.org/English/

AboutUs/AboutUs/200802/english_21410.html; accessed February 11, 2012.

8. Liu Xiaobo, a prominent independent intellectual in China, is a long-time advocate of political reform and human rights in China and an outspoken critic of the Chinese communist regime; Liu has been detained, put under house arrest and imprisoned many times for his writing and activism. According to his lawyers' defense statement in his 2009 trial, Liu has written nearly 800 essays, 499 of them since 2005. Liu is a drafter and a key proponent of Charter 08.

Liu was born on December 28, 1955 in Changchun, Jilin. He received a BA in literature from Jilin University, and an MA and PhD from Beijing Normal University, where he also taught.

In April 1989, he left his position as a visiting scholar at Columbia University to return to Beijing to participate in the 1989 Democracy Movement. On June 2, Liu, along with Hou Dejian, Zhou Duo, and Gao Xin, went on a hunger strike in Tiananmen Square to protest martial law and appeal for peaceful negotiations between the students and the government. In the early morning of June 4, 1989, the four attempted to persuade the students to leave Tiananmen Square. After the crackdown, Liu was held in Beijing's Qincheng Prison until January 1991, when he was found guilty of "counter-revolutionary propaganda and incitement" but exempted from punishment.

In 1996, he was sentenced to three years of Reeducation-Through-Labor on charges of "rumor-mongering and slander" and "disturbing social order" after drafting the "Anti-Corruption Proposals" and letters appealing for official reassessment of the June Fourth crackdown.

On December 8, 2008, Liu was taken away from his Beijing home and detained by the Beijing police, and on December 25, 2009, more than a year later; he was found guilty of "inciting subversion of state power." By early March 2010, more than 600 co-signatories of Charter 08 signed an online "statement of shared responsibility" with Liu for his "crime."

Liu served as President of the Independent Chinese PEN Centre from 2003 to 2007. In addition to Columbia University, he was a visiting scholar at the University of Oslo and the University of Hawaii. Nobel Prize 2010, Liu Xiaobo; http://www.nobelprize.org/nobel_prizes/peace/laureates/2010/xiaobo.html; accessed February 11, 2012.

9. The Human Rights in China (HRIC) press statement and English translation of Yu Jie's statement were originally released on January 18, 2012, by HRIC (http://www.hrichina.org/content/5778), reprinted with permission from HRIC and Yu Jie. HRIC is an international Chinese human rights NGO based in Hong Kong and New York (http://www.hrichina.org/). Human Rights in China; http://www.hrichina.org/content/5778; accessed February 10, 2012.

10. Ibid.

Chapter 4

1. http://www.state.gov/j/drl/rls/irf/2010/148786.htm#; accessed May 8, 2012.

2. Ernesto Londono, "Afghan man, detained for being Sikh, is released from prison"; http://www.washingtonpost.com/blogs/blogpost/post/afghan-man-detained-for-being-sikh-is-released-from-prison/2012/02/01/gIQAbEdmhQ_blog.html; accessed February 11, 2012.

3. Lianne Gutcher, "Justice for Sahar Gul," *The Independent;* http://www.independent.co.uk/news/world/asia/justice-for-sahar-gul-afghan-family-who-tortured-child-bride-jailed-for-10-years-7718696.html; accessed May 8, 2012.

4. Visit http://parlvu.parl.gc.ca/ParlVu/ContentEntityDetailView.aspx?ContentEntityId=6958 for the full testimony.

Chapter 5

1. Israel Ministry of Foreign Affairs; http://www.mfa.gov.il/MFA/Facts percent20About percent20Israel/History/Facts

percent20About percent20Israel- percent20History; accessed February 12, 2012.

2. The Iranian Threat; http://www.mfa.gov.il/mfa/the percent20iranian percent20threat/overview/; accessed February 12, 2012.

3. Israel Ministry of Foreign Affairs; http://www.mfa.gov.il/MFA/Government/Communiques/2011/PM_Netanyahu_terrorist_attack_Itamar_12-Mar-2011.htm; accessed February 12, 2012.

4. Canadian Parliamentary Coalition to Combat Anti-Semitism; Evidence; November 30, 2009; Chair: Mario Silva; Parliamentary Publications; http://www.cpcca.ca/09.11.30transcript-E.pdf.

Chapter 6

1. Iran hosts 'The World without Zionism'; October 26, 2005; http://www.jpost.com/MiddleEast/Article.aspx?id=2906; accessed March 27, 2012.

2. http://gadebate.un.org/sites/default/files/gastatements/66/IR_en.pdf; accessed February 12, 2012.

3. Katherine Weber, "Youcef Nadarkhani 'Offended Islam' by Preaching Christianity"; *The Christian Post;* http://global.christianpost.com/news/youcef-nadarkhani-offended-islam-by-preaching-christianity-71496/; accessed March 28, 2012. See also www.christianpost.com.

4. Ibid.

5. http://mohabatnews.com/index.php?option=com_content&view=article&id=4094:arrest-of-a-number-of-christian-converts-in-a-house-church-in-kermanshah&catid=36:iranian-christians&Itemid=279; accessed May 8, 2012.

6. Iranian Security Authorities Arrested 10 Christian Converts; http://www.rescuechristians.org/index.php/2012/02/12/iranian-security-authorities-arrested-10-christian-converts/; accessed February 12, 2012.

7. Michael Carl, "Persecution of Christians Soars in Iran"; *World-NetDaily*, February 12, 2012; http://www.wnd.com/2012/02/persecution-of-christians-soars-in-iran/; accessed February 13, 2012.

8. MSN, "23 Hurt as Car Bomb Explodes near Iraqi Church, Two Other Attacks on Christians foiled"; http://www.msnbc.msn.com/id/43982676/ns/world_news-mideast_n_africa/t/hurt-car-bomb-explodes-near-iraqi-church-two-other-attacks-christians-foiled; accessed March 27, 2012.

9. Edwin Mora, "Obama Hails 'New Iraq,' But Ignores Persecution of Christians and Other Religious Minorities"; *CNS News*, December 13, 2011; http://cnsnews.com/news/article/obama-hails-new-iraq-ignores-persecution-christians-and-other-religious-minorities; accessed February 13, 2012.

10. United States Commission on International Religious Freedom, "USCIRF Letter to President Obama on Iraq"; http://www.uscirf.gov/news-room/press-releases/3678-uscirf-letter-to-president-obama-on-iraq.html; accessed March 27, 2012.

11. Ibid.

12. U.S. State Department Report on Iraq; http://www.state.gov/documents/organization/171735.pdf; accessed March 27, 2012.

13. Ibid.

Chapter 7

1. Ibrahim Garba and Jon Gambrell with Salisu Rabiu, *My Way News*, January 21, 2012, "At least 143 killed in north Nigeria sect attacks"; http://apnews.myway.com/article/20120121/D9SDE2S80.html; accessed February 2, 2012.

2. Joseph DeCaro, "Police persecute Christians in Sudan"; *Worthy News*, January 25, 2012; http://www.christianpersecution.info/index.php?view=11183; accessed February 15, 2012.

Chapter 8

1. *Pakistan Penal Code*, (XLV OF 1860), c. 15, s. 295-C., online: http://www.unhcr.org/refworld/docid/485231942.html; accessed March 13, 2012.

2. Doug Bandow, "Target Pakistan for Religious Persecution"; *The American Spectator,* July 5, 2011; http://spectator.org/archives/2011/07/05/target-pakistan-for-religious/; accessed February 15, 2012.

3. Mission to save a persecuted family; CTV News W5; March 13, 2010; http://www.ctv.ca/CTVNews/WFive/20100311/w5_saving_neha_100311/; accessed January 5, 2012. CTV W5 is Canada's most-watched documentary-newsmagazine program.

Appendix B

1. *Universal Declaration of Human Rights,* GA Res. 217(III), UN GAOR, 3d Sess., Supp. No. 13, UN Doc. A/810 (1948).

2. *International Covenant on Civil and Political Rights,* 19 December 1966, 999 UNTS 171, online: Office of the United Nations High Commissioner for Human Rights http://www2.ohchr.org/english/law/ccpr.htm accessed 12 November 2011.

3. U.S. Const. amend. I.

4. U.S. Const. art. VI.

5. U.S., Bill H.R. 2431, *International Religious Freedom Act of 1998,* 105th Cong., 1998, § 2(a)(1) (enacted) [*IRFA*].

6. "Remarks by the President on a New Beginning at Cairo University, Cairo, Egypt", 4 June 2009, online: The White House, Office of the Press Secretary http://www.whitehouse.gov/the-press-office/remarks-president-cairo-university-6-04-09 accessed 12 November 2011 ["A New Beginning"] (emphasis added).

7. *Pakistan Penal Code,* (XLV OF 1860), c. 15, s. 295-C., online: http://www.unhcr.org/refworld/docid/485231942.html accessed 13 November 2011.

8. Remarks by Hillary Rodham Clinton, "Remarks at the Release of the 13th Annual Report on International Freedom", 13 September 2011, online: State Department http://www.state.gov/secretary/rm/2011/09/172254.htm accessed 12 November 2011.

9. *IRFA, supra* note 5 at §2.

10. *IRFA, supra* note 5 at § 101(c)(2).

11. It should be noted that the Bush administration also did not fill the position for a full year.

12. Sec. 301(i) of *IRFA* states: "It is the sense of the Congress that there should be within the staff of the National Security Council a Special Adviser to the President on International Religious Freedom, whose position should be comparable to that of a director within the Executive Office of the President. The Special Adviser should serve as a resource for executive branch officials, compiling and maintaining information on the facts and circumstances of violations of religious freedom (as defined in section 3 of the International Religious Freedom Act of 1998), and making policy recommendations. The Special Adviser should serve as liaison with the Ambassador-at-Large for International Religious Freedom, the United States Commission on International Religious Freedom, Congress and, as advisable, religious nongovernmental organizations." *IRFA, supra* note 5 at § 301(i).

13. *Ibid.* at § 402(b)(1)(A).

14. "A New Beginning", *supra* note 6.

15. *IRFA, supra* note 5 at § 402(b)(1)(A).

16. United States Commission on International Religious Freedom, *Annual Report 2011,* online: United States Commission on International Religious Freedom http://www.uscirf.gov/images/book%20with%20cover%20for%20web.pdf accessed 12 November 2011.

17. *IRFA, supra* note 5 at § 2(b).

18. *Ibid.* at § 405(a).

19. *The Foreign Assistance Act of 1961, as Amended,* Pub.L. No. 87-195, § 116(a), 75 Stat 424 (enacted September 4, 1961, 22 U.S.C. § 2151 et seq.) [*Foreign Assistance Act*].

20. *Ibid.* at § 116(c)(3).

21. *Iraq: EU Bilateral Trade and Trade with the World,* online: European Union http://trade.ec.europa.eu/doclib/docs/2006/september/tradoc_113405.pdf accessed 11 November 2011.

22. Jeremy M. Sharp, *U.S. Foreign Assistance to the Middle East: Historical Background, Recent Trends, and the FY2010 Request,* 17 June 2009, online: USAID http://pdf.usaid.gov/pdf_docs/PCAAB954.pdf accessed 12 November 2011.

23. *Egypt,* online: Foreign Assistance.Gov http://foreignassistance.gov/OU.aspx?OUID=165&FY=2012 accessed 12 November 2011.

24. Bureau of Resource Management, *FY 2012 State and USAID—Core Budget,* online: State Department http://www.state.gov/s/d/rm/rls/fs/2011/156553.htm accessed 12 November 2011.

25. Interview with Secretary of State Hillary Rodham Clinton, "Interview with Sharif Amer of Al-Hayat TV", 29 September 2011, online: State Department http://www.state.gov/secretary/rm/2011/09/174882.htm accessed 12 November 2011.

26. *Foreign Assistance Act, supra* note 19 at § 502B(2).

27. *IRFA, supra* note 5 at § 405(a).

28. White House Office of the Press Secretary, "Statement by the Press Secretary on Violence in Egypt," 10 October 2011, online: White House http://www.whitehouse.gov/the-press-office/2011/10/10/statement-press-secretary-violence-egypt accessed 12 November 2011.

29. State Department Office of the Spokesperson, "Secretary Clinton's Call with Egyptian Foreign Minister Mohamed Kamel Amr", 11 October 2011, online: State Department http://www.state.gov/r/pa/prs/ps/2011/10/175236.htm accessed 12 November 2011.

30. Remarks by Secretary of State Hillary Rodham Clinton, "Remarks with Hungarian Prime Minister Viktor Orban", 30 June 2011, online: State Department http://www.state.gov/secretary/rm/2011/06/167374.htm accessed 12 November 2011.

31. Interview by Secretary of State Hillary Rodham Clinton, "Secretary Clinton's Interview with Sharif Amer of Al-Hayat TV", 1 October 2011, online: http://translations.state.gov/st/english/texttrans/2011/10/20111001163846su9.648639e-02.html accessed 12 November 2011.

32. "Remarks with Hungarian Prime Minister Viktor Orban," *supra* note 30.

33. "Freedom and Justice Party Open to Copt as Deputy," online: IkhwanWeb (Official English Site of the Muslim Brotherhood) http://www.ikhwanweb.com/article.php?id=28554 accessed 12 November 2011.

34. *Strategic Framework Agreement for a Relationship of Friendship and Cooperation between the United States of America and the Republic of Iraq,* United States and Iraq, 17 November 2008, online: State Department http://www.state.gov/documents/organization/122076.pdf accessed 12 November 2011 [*Strategic Framework Agreement*].

35. See Secretary Clinton's statement: "With the new government in place, we look forward to expanding our economic and security relationship, promoting cooperation on science, education, and health, strengthening the rule of law and transparent governance, deepening our cultural exchanges, and *improving our partnership in all the areas laid out in our Strategic Framework Agreement*" (emphasis added). Press Statement by Secretary of State Hillary Rodham Clinton, "Announcement of New Iraqi Government," 21 December 2010, online: Secretary of State http://www.state.gov/secretary/rm/2010/12/153423.htm accessed 12 November 2011. See also *Iraq,* online: Foreign Assistance.Gov http://foreignassistance.gov/OU.aspx?OUID=167&FY=2012 accessed 12 November 2011 ("the Strategic Framework Agreement between the United States and the GOI will continue to guide the relationship between the two nations").

36. *Security Framework Agreement, supra* note 34 at § IV(5).

37. *Iraq, supra* note 35.

Appendix C

1. *The Constitution of the Islamic Republic of Pakistan,* National Assembly of Pakistan (as modified 20 April 2010) at art. 20, online: http://www.mohr.gov.pk/constitution.pdf accessed 9 March 2012.

2. *The Constitution of the Islamic Republic of Pakistan,* National Assembly of Pakistan (as modified 20 April 2010) at art. 227(1), online: http://www.mohr.gov.pk/constitution.pdf accessed 9 March 2012.

3. *Pakistan Penal Code,* (XLV OF 1860), c. 15, s. 295-C., online: http://www.unhcr.org/refworld/docid/485231942.html accessed 13 March 2012.

4. United States Department of State, *International Religious Freedom Report: Pakistan, July-December 2010,* online: Department of State http://www.state.gov/documents/organization/171759.pdf accessed 13 March 2012.

5. *Ibid.*

6. Barnabus Fund, "Estimated 700 Christian Girls Annually Kidnapped and Forcibly Married to Captors in Pakistan," 19 September 2011, online: http://barnabasfund.org/UK/News/Archives/Estimated-700-Christian-girls-annually-kidnapped-and-forcibly-married-to-captors-in-Pakistan.html accessed 15 March 2012.

7. United States Department of State, *Trafficking in Persons Report 2011,* online: http://www.state.gov/j/tip/rls/tiprpt/2011/164233.htm accessed 13 March 2012.

8. United States Department of State, *International Religious Freedom Report, July-December 2010,* online: Department of State http://www.state.gov/j/drl/rls/irf/2010_5/168240.htm accessed 15 March 2010.

9. All references to the constitution of Afghanistan are to: *The Constitution of Afghanistan,* ratified 26 January 2004, online: *The Afghan Constitution,* January 4, 2004, online: http://www.afghanembassy.com.pl/cms/uploads/images/Constitution/The%20Constitution.pdf accessed 14 March 2012.

10. Office of the High Commissioner for Human Rights, "A Long Way to Go: Implementation of the *Elimination of Violence Against Women* Law in Afghanistan," November 2011, at p. 1, online: http://www.ohchr.org/Documents/Countries/AF/UNAMA_Nov2011.pdf accessed 13 March 2012.

11. For an overview of the impugned provisions of the law, see UN Human Rights Council, "Report of the Special Rapporteur on Freedom of Religion and Belief," 16 February 2010, A/HRC/13/40/Add.1, at p. 4-5, online: http://www2.ohchr.org/english/bodies/hrcouncil/docs/13session/A-HRC-13-40-Add1_EFS.pdf accessed 14 March 2012. See also Human Rights Watch, *World Report 2010: Afghanistan,* online: http://www.hrw.org/sites/default/files/related_material/afghanistan.pdf accessed 14 March 2012.

12. The guidelines were published on President Karzai's website at Office of the President of the Islamic Republic of Afghanistan, "Full Text of the Ulema Council," 2 March 2012, online: http://president.gov.af/fa/news/7489 accessed 14 March 2012.

13. Excerpt of statement on Eurasianet.org, "Karzai Backs Afghan Clerics Over Stronger Restrictions on Women," 8 March 2012, online: http://www.eurasianet.org/node/65105 accessed 15 March 2012.

14. All references to the Ulema Council declaration are to an unofficial translation adopted by the major media outlets: see "English translation of Ulema Council's declaration about women," Afghanistan Analysis Group, online: https://afghanistananalysis.wordpress.com/2012/03/04/english-translation-of-ulema-councils-declaration-about-women/ accessed 14 March 2012.

15. For a synopsis of the PBS special and a transcript of the interview with Under-Secretary General Coomaraswamy, see "The Dancing Boys of Afghanistan," 20 April 2010, online: http://www.pbs.org/wgbh/pages/frontline/dancingboys/etc/synopsis.html accessed 15 March 2012. Other news agencies or sources that have addressed the subject include Reuters, *The Guardian,* and CNN, among others.

16. M. Mati, "Officials: Taliban executes boy, 7, for spying" CNN, 10 June 2010, online: CNN http://www.cnn.com/2010/WORLD/asiapcf/06/10/afghanistan.child.execution/index.html accessed 15 March 2010.

17. "Remarks by the President on a New Beginning at Cairo University, Cairo, Egypt", 4 June 2009, online: The White House, Office of the Press Secretary http://www.whitehouse.gov/the-press-office/remarks-president-cairo-university-6-04-09 accessed 12 March 2012 ["A New Beginning"].

18. U.S., Bill H.R. 2431, *International Religious Freedom Act of 1998*, 105th Cong., 1998, at § 402(b)(1)(A) (enacted) [*IRFA*].

19. *Ibid.* at § 2(b).

20. *Ibid.* at § 405(a).

21. *The Foreign Assistance Act of 1961, as Amended*, Pub.L. No. 87-195, § 116(a), 75 Stat 424 (enacted September 4, 1961, 22 U.S.C. § 2151 et seq.) [*Foreign Assistance Act*].

22. *Ibid.* at § 116(c)(3).

23. As reported in the New York Times: see Steven Lee Myers, "Despite Rights Concerns, U.S. Plans to Resume Egypt Aid," 15 March 2012, online: http://www.nytimes.com/2012/03/16/world/middleeast/us-military-aid-to-egypt-to-resume-officials-say.html?r=1&hp# accessed 16 March 2012.

24. U.S., Bill H.R. 2055, *Consolidated Appropriations 2012*, 112th Congress, § 7041(a)(1)(B) (enacted 23 December 2011).

25. See §7041(a)(1)(C).

26. For a copy of the testimony, see Rev. Majed El Shafie, "Religious Freedom in Egypt and Iraq: A Statement Before the Subcommittee on Africa, Global Health, and Human Rights of the US. House of Representatives Committee on Foreign Affairs," 17 November 2011, online: http://foreignaffairs.house.gov/112/els111711.pdf accessed 16 March 2012.

27. *Pakistan,* online: Foreign Assistance.Gov http://foreignassis-tance.gov/OU.aspx?OUID=169&FY=2012&AgencyID=0&budTab=tab_Bud_Planned accessed 12 March 2012.

28. *Afghanistan,* online: Foreign Assistance.Gov http://foreignas-sistance.gov/OU.aspx?OUID=166&FY=2012&AgencyID=0&budTab=tab_Bud_Planned accessed 12 March 2012.

29. Based on figures from the Central Intelligence Agency, *CIA World Factbook: Afghanistan,* online: https://www.cia.gov/library/publications/the-world-factbook/geos/af.html accessed 14 March 2012.

30. U.S. Census Bureau, "Trade in Goods with Pakistan," online: http://www.census.gov/foreign-trade/balance/c5350.html accessed 14 March 2012.

31. *Pakistan: EU Bilateral Trade and Trade with the World,* 10 January 2012, online: European Union http://trade.ec.europa.eu/doclib/docs/2006/september/tradoc_113431.pdf accessed 14 March 2012.

32. U.S. Census Bureau, "Trade in Goods with Afghanistan," online: http://www.census.gov/foreign-trade/balance/c5310.html#2011 accessed 14 March 2012.

33. *Afghanistan: EU Bilateral Trade and Trade with the World,* 10 January 2012, online: European Union http://trade.ec.europa.eu/doclib/docs/2006/september/tradoc_114134.pdf accessed 14 March 2012.

ABOUT MAJED EL SHAFIE

Reverend Majed El Shafie, Founder and President of One Free World International (OFWI), was born in Egypt to a prominent Muslim family of judges and lawyers. He was detained and severely tortured by Egyptian authorities after he converted to Christianity and began advocating equal rights for Egyptian Christians. Sentenced to death, Rev. El Shafie fled Egypt by way of Israel and settled in Canada in 2002, establishing OFWI to share a message of freedom, hope, and tolerance for religious differences and to promote human rights in this area through advocacy and public education.

OFWI organizes conferences and other events which attract prominent Canadian politicians as keynote speakers. Through OFWI, Rev. El Shafie advocates on behalf of religious minorities globally, including Christians, Jews, China's Uyghur Muslims, Bahá'í's, Ahmadiyya Muslims, and Falun Gong, among others, and he has met with political and religious leaders in Pakistan, Afghanistan, Cuba, Israel, and Iraq to address minority rights. He is frequently called on to provide expert testimony in refugee and protection proceedings in Canada and the United States and has testified three times before the Sub-Committee on International Human Rights of the Canadian parliament's Standing Committee on Foreign Affairs and International Development as well as the Canadian Parliamentary Coalition to Combat

Antisemitism's inquiry into antisemitism in Canada. OFWI's other activities include assisting disadvantaged communities in Africa, the Middle East, and Asia with humanitarian aid and by helping them to build schools, hospitals, and orphanages.

More information is available through:

One Free World International/El Shafie Ministries

20 Bloor Street East, Box 75129
Toronto, Ontario M4W 3T3
Canada

Tel: 1 416 436 6528

Fax:

Email: info@onefreeworldinternational.org

Internet: www.onefreeworldinternational.org

~~~~~~~~~~~~~~~~~~~~~

Rev. El Shafie's work has been featured in many leading North American news media, including magazines, newspapers, radio, and television, and has recently been the subject of a feature-length documentary. Some of the Canadian national media to cover his work since 2005 include the Whistleblower Report of CTV National News, CTV's W5 newsmagazine, Canada AM, CBC television and radio news, and The Source. In print his work has been covered in the National Post, the Globe and Mail, the Ottawa Citizen, the Toronto Star, and the Toronto Sun, among others.

One Free World International

You can join One Free World International's alert network by visiting our website at www.onefreeworldinternational. org or by sending an email to info@onefreeworldinterna-tional.org. You can also like us on Facebook at www.facebook.

com/OneFreeWorldInternational or follow us on Twitter at @ MajedElShafie.

The work of One Free World International is wholly supported through the voluntary donations of our friends and members. These donations are not tax deductible because we choose to pursue the dream free of the legal restrictions placed on charities.

U.S. residents wishing to make a significant donation and requiring a tax receipt can contact us at info@onefreeworldinternational.org for information on how to donate.

If you would like to share in the dream in this manner, you may send your contribution to:

One Free World International

20 Bloor Street East, Box 75129
Toronto, ON
M4W 3T3

Or Direct Deposit to:

Bank: Toronto Dominion Bank

Institution Code: 004

Transit Number: 12492

Account Number: 1249 5002036 (Canadian deposits); 1249 7200215 (U.S. dollar deposits)

Swift: TDOMCATTTOR

IN THE RIGHT HANDS, THIS BOOK WILL CHANGE LIVES!

Most of the people who need this message will not be looking for this book. To change their lives, you need to put a copy of this book in their hands.

> *But others (seeds) fell into good ground, and brought forth fruit, some a hundred-fold, some sixty-fold, some thirty-fold* (Matthew 13:8).

Our ministry is constantly seeking methods to find the good ground, the people who need this anointed message to change their lives. Will you help us reach these people?

> *Remember this—a farmer who plants only a few seeds will get a small crop. But the one who plants generously will get a generous crop* (2 Corinthians 9:6).

EXTEND THIS MINISTRY BY SOWING
3 BOOKS, 5 BOOKS, 10 BOOKS, OR MORE TODAY,
AND BECOME A LIFE CHANGER!

Thank you,

Don Nori Sr., Founder
Destiny Image
Since 1982